BLESSINGS
IN THE
WAKE
of
GRIEF

By
THELMA GARCIA VILLENA

Villena Publishing

VILLENA PUBLISHING
4498 Sweet Shrub Court
Concord, California

Thelma Garcia Villena
Copyright © 2021 Thelma Garcia Villena

Published by Villena Publishing,
located at 4498 Sweet Shrub Court, Concord, California

ISBN: 978-1-7370170-2-8 paperback
ISBN: 978-1-7370170-3-5 ebook
Library of Congress Control Number: 2021922747

First Edition

Book Production and Publishing by Brands Through Books
brandsthroughbooks.com

To my beloved husband Flor, who has loved me more than I deserved and helped me to hold on to God's promises in times of fear and the agony of defeat.

You have the power to show that our home is safe, covered with peace, and protected by your undying love.

To my children, Melissa, V.J., and Iza: I want you to know that raising you on my own was the greatest blessing and joy in my life. Looking back, I do not know how I did it. I am so grateful to God for allowing me to be your parent. I love you so much.

To my sons-in-law and daughter-in-law, Eddie, Jenny, and Julien: I want you to know that I love you all like my own and am so grateful for every one of you. You all add value to my life. I am beyond blessed to have you all in my life.

To all my grandchildren, the crown of my age, without whom this book would not be possible: Nolan V. Lozano, Kailyn V. Lozano, Karyssa V. Lozano, Jordyn D. Villena, Jace V. Zhivago, Talia V. Zhivago, and Selah V. Zhivago. You have helped make my life beautiful. May your dreams all come true.

To my parents, Timoteo and Agueda Garcia: Thank you for being my parents and for instilling the love and trust for God at an early age. Thank you for your love and guidance. Thank you for your legacy of love.

To my Tatay and Inay Villena, who both poured their blessings into my life and the lives of my children. We are forever grateful.

To my sister, Luz and brother-in-law Angel: Thank you for helping me not only walk but run in my life's struggles.

To my sister Benigna and brother-in-law Bartolome: I could never thank you enough for all you have done for my family and me. I am grateful for all your love.

To Elizabeth and Sonny Garcia: Thank you so much for all the love and support you give to my children. We are all forever grateful.

To Lita and Allan Conception: I am grateful for the support in all of our endeavors.

To my Villena sisters and brothers in my heart: Thank you all for your continuous love and support for my family. We love you all dearly.

Contents

Note to Reader

Japanese Occupation of the Philippines

THE JAPANESE OCCUPATION of the Philippines occurred between 1942 and 1945 when Imperial Japan occupied the Commonwealth of the Philippines during World War II.

Japan occupied the Philippines until the surrender of Japan. A highly effective guerilla campaign by Philippine resistance forces allowed the guerrillas to control sixty percent of the islands, mostly mountain and jungle areas. Filipinos remained loyal to the United States, partly because of the American guarantee of independence and also because the Japanese had pressed large numbers of Filipinos into work details and even put young Filipino women into brothels.[1]

Japanese Rules for Filipinos During the Occupation

During the Japanese occupation, according to the author's mother, the Japanese ruled the Philippines with an iron hand. They declared martial law, enforced a strict curfew, and instilled fear by punishing and killing people who opposed them. They prohibited singing the national anthem and the

---

[1] Wikipedia contributors, "Japanese occupation of the Philippines," *Wikipedia, The Free Encyclopedia,* https://en.wikipedia.org/w/index.php?title=Japanese_occupation_of_the_Philippines&oldid=1049115307 (accessed October 11, 2021).

raising of the flag. Schools, printing presses, and radio stations were closed. The Japanese controlled everything.

Some of the rules the Japanese enforced during their regime include the following:[2]

1. Salute the Japanese soldiers when you meet them.
2. The Japanese flag must be displayed at the door of every house.
3. Everyone must wear the Rising Sun armband on the left arm.
4. Everyone must have a certificate of residence.
5. Whenever you see Japanese soldiers, you must welcome them and not try to escape or you will be considered an enemy.
6. No walking between sunset and sunrise without a lamp. The Japanese will shoot you without a warning if they see you without a lamp.

Makabayang Katipunan ng Ligang Pilipino (Makapili)

Of all the groups that collaborated with Japan during World War II, Makapili became the most infamous and hated.

Headed by the triumvirate of former Revolutionary General Artemio Ricarte, Pio Duran, and former Sakdalista Movement founder Benigno Ramos, the Makapili came into existence after the Japanese started to conscript Filipinos to augment their military forces. However, its members became feared not because of their fighting prowess but because of their treacherous behavior, which included spying and selling out their own people.

Whenever a village or a town was suspected of guerrilla activity, the Japanese would round up the residents and then let the Makapili members — who covered their faces with bamboo baskets except for their eyes — point out the suspected guerrillas or their sympathizers. In this way, many Filipinos,

---

[2] Japanese Rules for Filipinos in Manila, Philippines in WWII, 1941-5, www.reddit.com/r/HistoryPorn/comments/2gxuf6/japanese_rules_for_filipinos_in_manila (accessed October 11, 2021).

including those who were innocent, were dragged off by the Japanese to be tortured and executed.[3]

Tagalog Terms for Family Members

Anak: child, son/daughter

Ate: older sister

Inay: mother

Itay: father

Kuya: older brother

Lolo: grandfather

Nanay: mother (synonym for inay)

Ninong: godfather

Tatay: father

Tiya: aunt

---

[3] "10 Most Infamous Traitors in Philippine History," https://filipiknow.net/traitors-in-philippine-history (accessed October 11, 2021).

CHAPTER 1

Yes, I Have a Story to Tell

*Writing a memoir is like opening
up a life that has been dormant.*

— Cally Berryman

SOMETIMES I DESIRE TO TAKE away the veil of the golden age to get a glimpse of the soul underneath, the maiden she was all those years ago. Then I realize I don't have to. All I need to do is be attentive to her words and watch her beam, read her story, look at her eyes, and know and feel that she is still there as much as before when she was young once upon a time. I am sure under those silver hairs, there is prudence that only pain can endure and the heart remembers.

It is a great day under the solstice sun. I feel the warmth of the brilliant rays on my face. I say goodbye to the frosty breeze that brings cold creeping down the back of my neck and gives me goosebumps. I sit here watching the kids playing and making sandcastles on the beach, looking so happy — no worries, just enjoying the sand and water. I enjoy listening to one wave splash and then another, and then I watch it sparkle like bubbles on a gentle breeze. I close my eyes and listen to the laughter of the children. And I let the sunshine fall on my skin. I recall my childhood days and smile. As I sit here, I cannot help but go down memory lane, back to when I was on cloud nine, floating on air. I picture my brothers and myself playing, dancing in the boundless meadow in the middle of summer, and the river where we used to go to. I have a memory of my grandma cooking those fantastic foods she made just for us.

In my mind, I see a young girl about six years old with natural glowing lips and baby soft, rosy cheeks, and long, black hair braided in a single pigtail. She amused herself by playing dress-up using her mother's heels and big sisters' skirts. She ate without feeling the need to glance in the mirror. She sang as if no one else was listening. She knew what she wanted even before birth. This little angel picked her family on Earth. She wanted eleven brothers and sisters, and she got them. That little girl was me, and somewhere in time, I lost her. I want her back. Where did she go?

Suddenly, I hear an inner voice say, "I am here, ready for you. I have never left you. Keep the memories alive. After all, through our memories, we can make a world more perfect than the universe. We can bring back to life those people who no longer exist."

I whisper, "Then help me remember."

"Yes, I will help you remember," the inner voice says, and I recall a quote by Kevin Horsley from his book *Unlimited Memory*: "Your memory is the glue that binds your life together; everything you are today is because of your amazing memory. You are a data-collecting being, and your memory is where your life is lived."

"Come hold my hand," the inner voice continues. "Let us jump into the memory lane together, you and me, for we are one. Yes, we are one under the veil of the golden age who has the heart to remember."

I come back to myself and continue to imagine the days gone by. Memories with glowing colors come whirling in as if the breeze is their treasured song, as if they are ever ready to mambo. Positive memories come as a confidant with a basket full of goodies, nourishing and kind, making me feel self-confident, sensible, well-adjusted, balanced, and in command, able to value each moment as a gift and perceive a bright future.

I was born July 17, 1941, in a general hospital in the Philippines, five months before World War II came to our country. My Aunt Seryang told me that my soul chose my parents while I was still a floating piece in heaven. When I asked, "Why?" my aunt said to me, "Because you love to have so many brothers and sisters."

I answered, "That is very true. I love every one of my siblings."

I said that because I genuinely love each and every one, although I don't know them well, mostly because of the differences in our ages. My parents showed us how to love each other. My family consisted of my mother (*Inay*), Agueda Rivera Garcia, and my father (*Itay*), Timoteo Julian Garcia, and we were twelve brothers and sisters. My classmates and friends would ask, "Thelma, are you sure they are your sisters and brothers? They are much older than you."

"Of course I am sure. I am the third youngest one; that's why they look older than me."

Those questions did not bother me. All I knew was that we were all family, and we cared for each other. We were actually a blended family. When my parents decided to marry, my father already had five children, and my mother had two. They had five children together, so we were twelve: Ka Asias, Ate Lunding, Ate Remy, Ate Bening, Kuya Marcial, Ate Del, Ate Luz, Kuya Francis, Kuya Lando, Thelma (me), Alfredo, and Timoteo. Some of my brothers and sisters were indeed much older than I, but who cares? I loved them all. Life was great growing up with all my sisters and brothers. I was the only girl at the end of the flock, so I got all of their attention.

I must have picked my parents because my parents truly loved us all. My mother was a woman ahead of her time. Energetic, full of life, loving, healthy, and happy. She was also creative; she designed clothes for the rich and famous. My mother came from a well-to-do family in Novaliches, Quezon City, in Metro Manila. Her ancestors owned a lot of land, but no one would have guessed at her family's vast wealth as she remained humble and charitable. She always had enough to share with anyone who came and asked for help.

My father was a good man and was always gentle and calm with his children as they were growing up. He was employed as a *tenedor delibro*, or certified public accountant, in San Juan, Rizal.

My parents made sure that their children, especially the girls, were educated in whatever field they wanted to go into. At the time we were growing up, girls were not expected to finish their education as they are today. Girls were only supposed to serve their husbands. Most rich people trained their daughters in the ways of keeping a good house as they were supposed to care for their husbands and children in the home. My mother did not like the idea of *not* educating her girls. Her relatives did not like her plan and often gave her a hard time about it. They would come to the house and rattle off a list of reasons as to why the girls should not go to school.

"Agueda, why do you send your girls to school? You are just wasting the money. The girls need to stay home and learn how to serve their husbands," the relatives would grumble.

"My girls need to learn like the men. I want them to know and prepare for life," my mother would say. "No one can take our education away from us, and the money and the lands will vanish if the girls don't know how to handle the money." Those conversations would go on for years, but my mother stood her ground.

My parents made sure all of their children had access to education. We became lawyers, accountants, nurses, dentists, and dental assistants, medical assistants, experts in business management, and an entrepreneur. My parents always told us that "education is the passage to progress," and for that, I am forever grateful. My parents motivated us to dream big, and daydreaming and being creative have been reassuring experiences for me. Using my imagination is a part of what strengthens me as I am bountiful in that way. When I am in that creative flow, I feel myself becoming stronger, slowly but surely.

I am so grateful to my parents for encouraging us to dream. I was born in hard times. Japan invaded the Philippines in December 1941, the year I was born. The Japanese occupation was a time of confusion and fear. Acts of torture, rape, and massacres, sometimes of whole villages, took place all over the country. My parents were geniuses in helping us through the nightmare. I don't remember much about the war, but I do remember the stories told to me. Every day, the memories of World War II — its horrendous scenes, its explosive impact, its moments of both trepidation and courage — rest in the hearts of those who endured its terror every day.

My mother told me that from 1942 to 1945, during the Japanese invasion and occupation of the Philippines, our family left the city to live in the province of Novaliches in Quezon City. My parents left the titles of their lands and homes, jewelry, and other valuables to their eldest son, Kuya Asias. My father told him, "Son, please keep all of these for us, and we will get them back as soon as we are safe."

His son replied, "Okay, Itay. I will take care of these until you come back."

"I need to take all the small kids to the province," my father announced. The older ones would stay in Manila with my eldest brother.

We left for the province to be safe, my father thought, but to his dismay, he found out that at times it was more threatening.

Our family ended up in the Province of Quezon City, seventeen miles from Manila. My mother described our place as being in the beautiful countryside where the sunbeams were bright but without the heat of late spring. The air was warmer and more fragrant. A long path led to a cloud forest where a beautiful house stood. That cloud forest seemed to say that God was ready to furnish us with a new work of art.

The path to the house was a stone path. The house's exterior had gone through many winters and storms, but the old wooden floors inside had been protected. It had belonged to an old friend of my father's who had passed away and left this house to him. My mother said that it was a woodland dream that was a pleasure to walk in and that we were lucky to have it. She said the most important thing was that "you know it has an underground hiding place where we can always go for safety" if needed.

That extensive underground room was where my brother and I stayed most of the time. My mother said to me, "You pray all the time in that room every night. Your brother Lando always gets mad because you pray only for the simplest food, like eggplant and anchovies, while your brother will pray for fried chicken."

"Hmm, I am a simple girl," I whispered to myself.

I was so young then that I have only the stories that people tell me to rely on. My mother told me that she and my father lived in fear every day — fear for us children, fear for the adult children who were not with us, and fear for their own lives too. That underground room, my mother said, sheltered us from many scenes of violence and protected us from all the bombings and gunfire in the area. For that, I am so grateful.

CHAPTER 2

My Mother's Fierce Fight to Save My Father

*Faith is unseen but felt, faith is strength when
we feel we have none, faith is hope
when all seems lost.*

— *Catherine Pulsifer*

LIFE HAS A WEIRD WAY of leading us to many avenues of different magnitudes. It sometimes guides our souls on throughways not traveled by others, maybe because our love and passion lead us there. Sometimes it will lead us to walk a certain road, not for ourselves but for the good of others. Some highways will lead us to discover new possibilities that will make our lives better. Life makes us pilgrims on these paths, giving rise to a more significant learning experience and greater wisdom. Remember that the track of our lives can change in an instant. During the Japanese occupation, my parents found themselves on one of life's avenues that was both extremely difficult and yet full of great possibilities. This is one of the many horrifying and soul-searing experiences still fresh in my mother's mind to this day. This is her story.

It was a rainy day. The rain came with a self-assured wind, invigorating the trees with its whirlpool of blowing rain. It also came with an angelic soundtrack as it cleansed every tint of color into a profound and robust vibrancy. The ground was mighty muddy and wet. Most families had stayed home that day because the rain was too much. It was a great day to relax and spend time with the family.

Loud shouting from the street suddenly disturbed the day's silence. "Makapili! Makapili is coming!" warned the boy as he ran from house to house. Makapili was the common name for Makakaliwa Katipunan Ñg Mg͂a Bayani, or the Alliance of Philippine Patriots, which was formed in 1944 by Benigno Ramos and Artemio Ricarte to help the Japanese army.

Makapili was, in the words of Ramos, a nationalist poet, "the creation of the Filipinos to suppress disorder, to awaken the misguided elements, to ameliorate the food problems of the people, and to aid the imperial Japanese forces and other Asian nations in the successful prosecution of the war." The existence of the Makapili made it difficult to tell who was a friend and who was a foe. Nothing was more terrifying than being betrayed by a poor or uneducated countryman whom the Japanese had recruited.

My parents were outside, feeding the horses they used to deliver goods to the vendors in Divisoria, Manila. They heard the loud cry of the boy shouting, "Makapili! Makapili!"

My *inay* (mother) immediately said to our helper, "Run to the house. Keep the children safe. Don't let them out for any reason. Hurry!"

"Yes, madam," the helper said and ran as fast as he could to the house to protect the children.

My parents hurriedly led the horses into the barn and nervously walked out to the street to see what was going on. They saw all the men in the neighborhood, looking puzzled and terrified, lined up on the road. My inay saw a man with his head covered so as not to be recognized, and she knew it meant trouble. The Makapilis were here. She glanced at my father standing close to her, and she was terrified. He was trembling with fear. His body seemed to have no vigor; his bones and muscles were lax, and he seemed to have lost any intent to fight. He was quiet.

"Oh my Jesus," my mother said silently. "What will happen to all of us here?" She thought of the beautiful life she had with my father, his gentleness, his love for her and for all of their children. He seemed to come more fully alive when he was with the children and loved them all the same.

My mother looked at this loving husband and father, still handsome but so scared. He looked at her tenderly, with steady breaths, which was more than enough to make her fall in love with him all over again. She thought of their marriage and the first day that they met. It seemed as though the universe had brought together two lovers who had already promised themselves to each other. Their union was a deep and devoted friendship, their passion so strong that each would have sacrificed anything for the other. They became soulmates as well as lovers. Their marriage was not a façade but a great bond of love and friendship and trust.

Early on, they both realized that love required commitment and attention and that happiness in love came from sharing not only the good times but also the bad. They both knew that love requires sacrifice in order to cultivate a relationship for mutual benefit.

Their fondness for each other was often envied by many of their acquaintances. Their love was real, and they understood it to be a guardian, an advocate, a tight connection that stayed with them always and in all ways. They both understood that the real love that they shared rejoiced with them, raised them up, was fine with their sadness and fear, and caressed the scars they hid from others. They learned to value their love and tried their best to keep it as long as they lived because they both realized that real love was the greatest blessing heaven can give.

"Yes, our love for each other has flourished through the years," my mother told us as she continued her story in her own words. "I didn't know what I would do if something happened to your father," she said. "He was still near me. No Japanese had taken notice of him yet. I prayed to the greatest God of all to please spare my husband from a terrible fate. I glanced at his thin body, and I saw his knitted brow and his furrowed forehead beaded with sweat. I could feel his body trembling with fear and apprehension. He was in a complete state of panic that almost threatened to unman him.

"I looked at the other men on the street. Some were very young — boys, really. Some were old and sickly, and some were strong, angry-looking men. I saw that all these men were helpless in the face of these heartless Japanese soldiers, who, with a flick of a machine gun trigger, would destroy them. I could not help but remember all of our relatives who became victims of the war. The Japanese took my Uncle Basilio one evening just to ask some questions. He never returned to my aunt. We later learned that the Japanese had killed him because he had refused to become part of the Makapili. My nephew Angel — so young, only seventeen years old, so fragile, so eager to help — was killed helping a woman being raped by a Japanese soldier. Killing heroes was what the Japanese did. Just feeling irked was enough incentive for them to fire bullets into the helpless resistors. They knew that there was no need to restrain the population directly; they just had to exploit their role models. They killed anyone who disobeyed them and rewarded those who took their money. The soldiers massacred the heroes but applauded the backstabbing villains.

"I stood there helplessly praying for mercy to my Almighty God of all mercy. I prayed as I had never prayed before. I prayed that our loved ones and their loved ones would be safe from harm. I even prayed for the Japanese soldiers so they could find mercy and be kind and learn the ways of the Lord. I prayed for mercy for not only my family but for all the families that were hoping for mercy during that trying moment. I prayed for strength and hope and faith in that moment of doubt and uncertainty. I thanked the Lord for being with us every day and every moment. Those prayers somehow helped me in those hours of misery. I prayed nonstop to ease the anxiety and fear. I prayed so hard, but resentment clouded my thoughts, and anger rippled through me. *Why did God let this happen?* I asked silently. My eyes flooded with tears, and my hands squeezed into fists while I took a sharp breath of frustration. My expression hardened, and I looked up toward heaven. *Please show pity on all of us. Help us all, my God Almighty.* I continuously rocked heaven above with unceasing prayers of mercy for all of us. I believed with all my heart that He was full of mercy, and I placed all hope in His mighty hands.

"A vast wall of gray clouds approached, and the apprehension grew ever so slightly with each passing moment. The warm afternoon slowly began its plunge into a fantastic breezy evening as the rain started to pour again. Across the wavy pasture, the flourish of trees on the edge of the woods came alive as they rocked back and forth, like stalks of rice from some lonely fields in Novaliches. The rain poured down on us as we stood on the road. We were not allowed to find shelter. We were soaked. The Japanese showed no mercy. The rain continued to pour. It was crazy. Those drops were bigger than a prairie cloudburst and coming down just as hard. The raindrops felt like they were hitting my eardrum. I found it relaxing. The summer flowers bent under their weight. This type of rain got everyone wet without filling the rain barrel. This type of rain got the streams running with pure water from the mountain. As the rain continued to pour, our bodies continued to tremble in fear, the kind of fear that feels like a dagger in the gut, slowly becoming entangled, or like a piercing rock constantly bashing our heads. It's not the predictable anger or pain that was the worst; it was the random stuff you know is coming, just not when.

"I was deep in my prayers when I heard the voice of a furious Japanese soldier. He was coming toward my husband and shouting, '*Bakayaro* (stupid bastard), come here! Come here quickly!'

"At that moment, the worst moment in the life of a mother and a wife, I felt like Heaven and Earth had fallen on me, and I could not breathe. I could only look up to heaven and hold on dearly to my faith, to the belief that something would happen or someone would be there for us. I knew everything right then was going wrong, but I had given it all to the Lord. I had done everything I could do. I just needed to trust.

"I grabbed my husband away from that cruel monster with all my might, shouting, 'Leave him alone! He is old and very sick!' I hung onto him, trying to protect him from the evil one. My pleading fell on the deaf ears of the terrorist, who continued to drag my husband away. I did not let go, even for a second. The heartless Japanese soldier continued to pull my husband away while I continued to hold him tight. I was dragged to the ground and covered with mud and dirt, but I never let go of him, pleading for them to let him go. I cried so much that the dirt and tears mixed to muddy my face, but I never let go. I continued to shout, 'Do not take him! You do not have any use for him! He is very sick!' My husband kept signaling me to save myself, but I did not listen. Instead, I held him tighter so that one bullet could kill us both. At that moment, we were on death row, and I did not care what happened to me. I believed in love, and at that moment, I was the protector. I was staying with my husband. I would never let him go with this bastard. The Japanese soldier dragged me and tried with all his might to make me let go, but he failed. Then all of a sudden, a Japanese officer came on the scene and said, "Let them both go. We do not have any use for them.' He let go, and we fled in a flash to hide. That very moment, I believed in miracles. A miracle came in my moment of need because I had faith.

"We found out later that the Japanese soldiers had pushed the remaining men into the truck, and they were tied and forced to wait for the Japanese to take them to the lumberyard, where they were stabbed and then shot. No one survived."

CHAPTER 3

Ate Remy Tends the Wounded

*A true hero isn't measured by the size of their strength,
but by the strength of their heart.*

— Zeus in Disney's *Hercules*

WAR IS EVIL, AND ITS terrors are many and of such a degree that they cannot be portrayed in words. In this war, there were a colossal number of murders and properties lost. Thousands became widows and orphans. War is the enemy of all humanity and human civilization.

My parents knew the destruction that war can bring, not only for our family but for all families. They knew that war was not a solution to problems, but, instead, it generated problems of all kinds. As soon as my father heard the war was coming, he decided to split up his children — at that time, there were ten of us — to get us to safety. My mother directed us thus: "The two small ones, Thelma and Lando, go with us to the province. The older ones, Lourdes and Remy, will stay with Asias. They will be safe in Manila. Luz will have to stay with the nuns; she will be safe there in the convent. Bening and Marcial will go to another relative in another province. Francis and Delia will stay in San Juan with other relatives."

My father attempted to pick up my sister Remy from the Philippine General Hospital, where she was studying nursing, but a hospital official told him, "It's safer here than in any other place. The hospital cannot be destroyed." My father tried, again and again, to pick her up, but hospital officials would not let her go, insisting that she would be safe there. He told us, "My plea was in vain."

At the hospital, Remy was able to help the sick and the dying. My mother was so worried and tried several times to get her back, but the officials did not let her out. At that point, inner peace seemed to be beyond my parents' reach. My mother remembered that "Remy really wanted to be a nurse, to serve the sick." Even as a small girl, she played the nurse to her brothers and sisters.

Remy had entered the School of Nursing at the Philippine General Hospital (PGH) in the fall of 1941 when war was just a rumor. For Remy, life was routine. She had an easy shift and learning was fun. On December 8, 1941, everything changed. Japanese bombs began raining down on the people of the Philippines. The nursing students tended to the most devastating injuries of war, those who had suffered the terrors of shells and shrapnel. The worst was yet to come.

For the first time in young Remy's life, she saw the casualties of brutal combat as injured bodies flooded into their wards. Remy, as young as she was, had to tend to the sick. "I cannot even weep or wail over these; I have to tend to the sick," she said as she told atrocious stories of horror. "Diseases like malaria and dysentery became commonplace, but we nurses stayed at our shift tending to the sick the best we could," she said.

Remy tended to the sick for the next three years. In 1945, her nightmare was finally over but only after days of fierce fighting between joint Filipino and American troops and the Japanese. Inside the hospital at that time were many Filipino patients and thousands of refugees seeking shelter there. There were few Japanese in the hospital, but Japanese soldiers were fortifying it on the outside.

A vivid account of the battle for the liberation of the hospital is the subject of Miguel P. Avanceña's article, "PGH 1945: Days of terror, nights of fear," published in the *Philippine Daily Inquirer* on February 18, 2012. Avanceña had been a young student at a school in Manila that was taken over by the

Japanese. He was then taken to De La Salle College for safety until that institution was closed, and he ended up seeking refuge at PGH. Here is a condensed version of his account:

> The battle for the liberation of the Philippine General Hospital on Taft Avenue in Manila was only one in the many series of street-to-street, house-to-house, and building-to-building fights that was the story of the liberation of the city in 1945. It was also one of the fiercest. . . .
>
> We had not imagined the Americans would shell the hospital, which was full of patients, staff, and refugees . . . who were told by the Japanese to stay indoors or be killed. . . . During that week, which never seemed to end, artillery barrages came crashing down on us in carpet-bombing fashion. . . . Some shells seemed to have a delayed-action fuse as these would shake the building first and explode a minute later, causing chaos. Patients and nurses were given the priority to sleep on the floor. The rest had to squat, remain standing or lean against the wall, sometimes for days. The doctors operated on the wounded without anesthesia, lights, and water. . . .
>
> The morning of Feb. 17 dawned on us brightly. We braced ourselves for the morning artillery barrage. The rapid staccato of "woodpecker" machine guns could be heard, backdropped by the rattle of musketry with occasional loud "whoomps" from bazookas or mortars.
>
> We were resigned to the thought that we would die before the Americans arrived. There was almost no food and water for the thousands trapped inside the hospital. A heavy barrage suddenly came crashing down on us, preceded by the all-too-familiar distant booming of cannons. Count six seconds and the shell would either hit you or fly overhead. By midmorning, the barrages came in quick succession. Machine-gun fire from both sides suddenly opened up in a deafening duel.

Heavy fire peppered the building with bullets without letup. There was a crash of exploding shells against concrete and the sound of ricocheting shrapnel and bullets. We were crouched under the elevator, but showers of sparks from exploding shells and shrapnel so terrified us that prayers asking God to save us filled the basement.

Then, as if by magic, all noise stopped. . . . After a deafening silence, we heard someone shout — then sing — "God Bless America."

Remy told us that when she saw the Americans, she said, "My, you are so big!" Then one soldier handed her a chocolate bar.

PGH had been liberated. My sister walked seventeen kilometers to get home to us. She missed three years of her life not knowing what was going on in the world. Remy's story was a triumph of the spirit in the face of hazardous adversity, a reminder of the preciousness of freedom.

Even to this day, memories of the battle for the liberation of the hospital remain in Remy's heart and soul. She recalls one of her worst nightmares. She said that one little boy about ten years old had asked her for a drink of water. She was so busy tending to others that when she came back to him, the sweet little boy was already dead. She cried for days.

Remy found out later on why the Americans had bombed the hospital. The Japanese had kept all civilians inside to trick the Americans into thinking that only Japanese were in the hospital.

On August 15, 1945, Japan finally surrendered. Battles have their heroes, sung and unsung. For many, their acts of bravery and heroism were known only to God. May they all rest in peace, embraced by the Almighty.

CHAPTER 4

Makapili Tortures Ka Asias

But war is also an incredible teacher.
A brutal instructor. We learned
a lesson in war written in blood,
about sorrows, loss, and pain.

— Jocko Willink

MY BROTHER ASIAS, A DENTIST who stayed in Manila because Manila was declared an open city during the Japanese occupation, was one of the many victims of the Makapili. As my mother tells the story, he was pretty well-known in his community and had a lot of friends as well as patients. His friends included the elites as well as the Japanese higher-ups. His family so far was doing well. My brother, according to my mother, was a good man. He was responsible and loved being a good brother to all of his siblings. Everybody loved and trusted him. He became a dentist at the young age of twenty-one and had a great clientele. Some folks wear a smile; Asias *was* a smile. Everything about him was a soft and understated joy. His patients went to him for treatment, but they got so much more. He was concerned about them. He asked about their day, their lives, and invited them to share their feelings. People wondered how many of his patients went on to become better friends, better bosses, better parents because of his care. He was the safest person around, one man spreading goodness. He was confident in who he was. One could sit and listen to him all day and smile. He was well-respected and loved in the community.

One night, a knock came on Ka Asias's door. The azure haze of the day had just lifted to reveal the stars shining like sugar spilled on black marble. Usually, the night sky is a welcome sight, surfacing like magic at each sunset, retreating at dawn's first light. But not tonight.

One knock on the door. Ka Asias asked, "Who is there?"

A voice faintly answered, "It's your friend. I am here to warn you. The Makapili are coming for you." The voice faded and was gone.

Ka Asias's chest suddenly tightened with fear. Terror twisted his gut, and he was unable to breathe. He looked at himself in the mirror and did not like what he saw. He had often wondered what would happen if these psychopathic invaders took over the world. And he knew that even if everyone did their best, many more people would die a horrible death. Now the threat was at his doorstep. Fear pierced his heart. He woke up his family: his wife, Loleng; six-year-old son, Paquito; four-year-old Norma; two-month-old Connie; and my sister, Lourdes. He led them downstairs to their shelter. "Stay here no matter what," he told them. "Never leave this place. You will all be safe here." His whole family, crying and trembling with fear, stayed in the shelter and quietly prayed for his life and theirs.

That night, Makapili pointed to my brother as the one who helped the movement against the Japanese. They tortured him so badly that he vomited blood. They showed no mercy. They left him to die. They ransacked his office and destroyed his property. Still, they were not able to get any information from him. He knew he had to keep silent, even when facing death, in order to protect the lives of all the people trying to defend his country.

Ka Asias survived the ordeal. He was found by friends who helped him after the Japanese left him to die. He got to live long enough to witness the liberation of the Philippines but died shortly thereafter due to injuries to his lungs caused by the torture the Japanese inflicted on him. He was thirty-three years old. My parents were devastated by the death of their firstborn son. Ka Asias promised my parents that he would take care of all of his brothers and sisters. Children are expected to live longer than their parents. My parents suffered from excessive loneliness and fear for the future. It was a horrible experience for the whole family. The loss of a son is carried in the heart of the parents forever.

One other horrifying incident in this war that touched my family was the massacre of the Christian Brothers.

De La Salle College in Manila was a Catholic school run by the Institute of the Brothers of the Christian Schools. The Christian Brothers had been friends to my family, and one day my mother told us the story of the massacre on the school campus.

As the war raged on in Manila, the school took in some people, families and others, with the hope that their being on the campus would isolate them from the bloodshed and destruction happening outside its grounds. Throughout the war, the school was allowed to operate even though the Japanese had taken over part of its campus. Some of the Christian Brothers were German, and because Germany was an ally of Japan, this gave them and the school a pass.

Sadly, the safety the Christian Brothers thought they could provide did not last.

On February 12, 1945, a group of Japanese soldiers forcibly made their way onto the campus. At that time, the school was giving refuge to almost seventy people, including thirty women, sixteen European Christian Brothers, and the school chaplain, Father Francis Cosgrave.

The arrival of the Japanese brought justified fear because the Japanese suspected that the people seeking shelter inside the campus were secretly helping the Americans. They herded them into the school's chapel and swiftly shot or stabbed them all, including the women and children.

At the end of the day, their bodies were found piled on top of each other. The chapel floors and walls were soaked with blood. It has been said that the blood seen on the walls was so extensive that it was not easily removed, and faint traces of it remain underneath the current paint job.

About forty-one civilians and sixteen Christian Brothers died that day. Those who survived, including Father Cosgrave, had to hide as they feared the Japanese would come back. They hid until the Americans freed them on Valentine's Day.

To this day, the events of February 12, 1945, remain a dark chapter in the history of De La Salle. The school has held Mass in the chapel every February 12th since the war in memory of the Christian Brothers and all the people who died that day.

War is never good. It destroys the very essence of humanity and produces constant and unrelenting fear. Let us seek peace instead.

CHAPTER 5

Back to Manila

Coming home is one of the most beautiful things.

— Andrei Rieu

ONE DAY OUT OF THE blue, my inay said, "Good news! The time has come to return to Manila."

"Manila?" I eagerly asked. "What is Manila? Where is Manila? I am five years old. I have not been anywhere except here."

My inay calmly said, "Yes, we are finally going back home. No more war. And you are all ready to go to school."

"School? I have never been to school," I said.

"You will be okay," my mother assured me. "We will start packing soon and leave for Manila next week. Don't worry. We can come and visit here too."

The day arrived for us to leave. I heard the steady patter of rain on my window, droplets sent to scatter the rays of the rising sun. The sound brought a calmness to my little mind, a soothing melody, a natural lullaby. With my eyes at rest, in those moments of solitude, I felt happy. The rain song fused with birdsong, bringing sweet, high notes. In my mind's eyes, I was a bird singing from up on the rooftops, filling my lungs with fresh air, watching the world come into focus. The early morning daylight unwrapped the hues of the world.

Then I heard my name. "Thelma, come eat your breakfast. We'll leave after the rain," my mother said.

Wow, we were going to Manila! I ran to the kitchen as fast as I could. The excitement fueled my engines with anticipation. The enthusiasm came like a skyrocket of electricity. The mission was to *go!* An inner ray of sunshine brightened my eyes and soul. I was so eager to see our future home.

Enthusiasm is undoubtedly part of the sugar of life as it acts as a magnifying lens for joy. My mother saw the glow in my eyes and said, "Thelma, eat your food. You will see our house in Manila soon."

"Is the house in Manila big, Inay?" I asked.

"Oh, yes. You will see that you will like it," my inay answered.

We rode a kalesa to Manila. This two-wheeled, horse-drawn carriage had been the primary mode of transportation, public or private, in the Philippines. However, its use declined after the war, giving way to motorized vehicles. My eyes sparkled as I took my first kalesa ride. I could see the horse making its great strides, carrying itself most elegantly. That horse was as gentle as a cat. It walked in a caring manner, and I felt that it would not hurt anyone. It felt good riding in the kalesa for the first time.

My mother sat beside me and tried her best to answer my question: *"Inay, where is Manila?"*

"Anak," she said softly, "Manila is about twenty kilometers from Quezon City, so riding on the kalesa will take longer. Manila used to be a great place." She continued to brief me about our destination.

Manila has been called the "Pearl of the Orient." The Pasig River divides the city into north and south. On the south side is the ancient walled city of Intramuros. On the north side is Escolta, the main business section.

As the country's capital, it was used in World War II for its port, airfields, towers, shipyards, and factories. When the war first broke out, Manila was taken by surprise and was captured. The Battle of Manila, between joint Filipino and American forces and the Japanese, from February 3 to March 3, 1945, cost more than 100,000 lives and caused massive destruction to the city.

Historian William Manchester wrote in *American Caesar*: "Seventy percent of utilities, 75 percent of factories, 60 percent of residential properties, and 100 percent of the business district were razed" in the course of the battle. The Japanese had used the residential buildings and public buildings as defense positions. In an article titled "When Manileños Died with Their City," Bambi Harper wrote: "The combatants took our history when they leveled Intramuros, they took our future when they slaughtered our youth."

The United States formally recognized Philippine independence on July 4, 1946, so my parents decided to come back to Manila to start a new life.

We arrived at our destination after a long ride. I watched my mother as she eagerly stepped out of the kalesa. She beamed at the sight of the house, her face radiant with joy. Inside, she lifted her eyes to the ceiling and cried. "I cannot believe we are finally home," she said. The terrible nightmare was over. It was as if the continuum of time had folded in on itself and was now being expressed as many, many petals of a beautiful flower. For my mother, coming home brought back to her a string of moments before the misery, all those precious ticks of the clock now adding up to an immense feeling of joy. At that moment, I saw an incredible look of happiness in my mother's eyes. That was such a wonderful sight.

That day was my first time coming to that house, so I feasted my eyes on its magnificent grandeur. It was so big that, according to what my mother told me, the Japanese had made it their headquarters, and the family had been forced to move out.

The housekeeper had cleaned the house before we came, so it looked good. And peaceful. Any traces of the Japanese who had lived there seemed to have vanished. It seemed there was a melody in the walls of that house that raised my spirit. In those quiet moments when the breeze became still and the Earth seemed to pause to take a minute to breathe, in that silent expression, I found a feeling of inner peace and realized that I was also home. Along with my inay, I looked up at the ceiling. "It's so high and spacious, I could fly a kite in here," I whispered to myself.

That house was my home, where laughter could start to happen. From the street, it was masonry and mortar, the same as any other. Yet when I stepped inside, I knew that it was different. It was a place where the lungs could fill a little more deeply and the heartbeat becomes a little steadier. It was a beautiful home. It had large, curved windows through which light flowed in all seasons, gracing the air, illuminating the sweet, toffee-brown wooden floor. The stairs leading up to the living room were grandeur themselves. They were laid one at a time, perhaps on one fine day. I wondered at their beauty and how magnificently they were made. That house was definitely made with love.

I rushed down to see the kitchen. It was spacious, and its wall tiles brought a honeycomb-yellow hue to the room, making it feel divine. "I will for sure enjoy breakfast and all the meals here," I said to my excited self. The dining room, which was adjacent to the kitchen, had a round table that seats eight. From both the kitchen and the dining room came the homiest aromas, the kind of fragrances that spoke directly to the best of our memories together. That beautiful house was a great place to make memories together, but unfortunately, most of my older siblings had gone away, either to school or jobs, and were no longer with us to make those memories.

The only ones left to live in this grandeur were my parents, my sister Lourdes (second to the oldest), my brother Lando, and me. My Ate Remy, an adventurer, left to experience new excitement in Guam. She was a good nurse and a good dancer. Ate Bening stayed with a nun to continue her studies. My Kuya Marcial, the wanderer, was in Batangas, trying to find whatever it was that he was looking for. Ate Del and Kuya Francis stayed in the dorms of Hospicio de San José, helping with the care of orphans while they went to school. Ate Luz was at St. Therese's High School and would come home on occasion. Alfredo and Timoteo had not yet been born. Alfredo was born in December 1946, and Timoteo, my father's junior — we called him "Sonny" — was born in August 1949.

I have one grim memory from my life in this beautiful place. While wandering around the house and its grounds, I happened to find sacks of Japanese money in the garage — blood-stained Japanese capital. It was useless, so my brother Lando and I made airplanes out of this worthless "treasure."

It was time to begin school, so my parents enrolled me at Pedro Guevarra Elementary School in Binondo, Manila. Education for all of their children — girls and boys, without exception — had been my parents' goal all their lives, and so far they had been successful as all of my brothers and sisters before me had attained the education they needed for their chosen professions. My family produced lawyers, a dentist, nurses, medical assistants, an accountant, an expert in business management, and an entrepreneur. My parents wanted their children to have the proper tools to deal with unpredictable life situations and believed with all their heart and soul that having an education would help us think, feel, and behave in a way that contributed to our success in life. My mother believed a good education would develop and improve our personalities, thoughts, self-esteem, and relationships with others. It would prepare us to face life with a clearer mind and help build our self-confidence, thus paving the way for us to succeed. She also believed it would help us overcome fear by viewing obstacles or new and frightening situations as challenges. My parents recognized this as a necessary tool in life and worked hard to educate their children. They stood their ground amid all the challenges they faced because they loved us and wanted us to be better contributors to the community where we lived. Those principles of education have been grounded in my mind ever since I was born, and I am so grateful.

I was excited to go to school for the first time but also scared. Cooped up in a shelter during the war, I never learned how to deal with people. The thought of talking to people terrified me.

Fighting back tears, I said to my mother, "Inay, I am scared to go to school. Can I go tomorrow instead?"

My mother hugged me and said, "You have to go today. The teacher will be looking for you."

"Please send our *yaya* to tell her I am not feeling well," I said with tears in my eyes. *Yaya* is a word for a helper or someone who takes care of others. Maggie was the name of our *yaya*. She took me to school and then picked me up and brought me home.

All the pleading and carrying on did not help. I still had to go to school.

The school was within walking distance of our house, so Maggie walked me to school. The bell had already rung when we arrived, so I found my class and went to my assigned area. To welcome newcomers like me on this first day of school, students in all of the grades higher than grade one linked their fingers together and made a welcoming archway, a tunnel of smiles for us to walk through. That benevolent gesture put me at ease and made me feel loved. What an unforgettable experience!

During the orientation, I found out that, in this school system, students stayed together for their entire school career. Because of this, they became like a family and didn't bully each other. Everyone in the room was a part of the school family, and as part of our education, we learned how to care for and protect one another. So thank God that on this day, my very first day in school, I became part of a new tribe that became the protective cocoon I needed to become a beautiful butterfly, the one that changes the world for the better with each simple flap of its wings.

CHAPTER 6

Finally, High School!

This school is not the million bricks, but the
thousand hearts who carry more dreams
than the night sky has stars. This school
is the emotions, our stories, and our love
for each other. I hope you can see that through
the stress-filled haze. . . We aren't the product;
we are the reason.

— Angela Abraham

THE YEAR WAS 1954, AND the day was very exciting. It was my first day of high school. I woke up early. The glowing morning glimmer was just peeking through the ocean of blue clouds, and the birds were singing their early rituals. A gentle breeze coming through my bedroom windows fell across my face. The golden light was everywhere, covering the Earth and its creations. Beauty and magic filled the air with the promise of a magnificent beginning.

My *yaya*, Maggie, had already prepared my uniform. Maggie had beautiful brown eyes, black hair down to her shoulders, and a cheerful personality. She was a teenager, about seventeen years old, and helped us in exchange for her education. She was an excellent and jolly worker. I heard her knock and her voice: "Thel, are you awake? Breakfast is ready."

"Yes, Maggie, I am awake. I will be there soon. Thank you," I said gently.

I immediately took a shower and put on my ironed uniform, which was white with a blue collar. I looked so cute in this uniform, my first. I met my sister Ate Lunding in the dining room, looking so happily at me. "Hey, Thel. You look like a *colegiala*." A *colegiala* is a student who goes to a private school for the rich.

I smiled and said, "Yes, Ate. This uniform makes me look rich."

"You better watch it," my sister said. "The boys might notice you. Inay won't like that."

"I know. Inay said no looking at the boys. Study first. Studying is your priority," I said to my sister, and we both giggled.

I was enrolled at Colegio de Jesus Maria in San Juan, Rizal. We were living at our house in Santa Lucia in San Juan. My sister Lourdes, who was now married with children, lived with us. My *inay* came home only on the weekends because she had a booming business in fashion design in Manila. She had twenty dressmakers creating beautiful dresses for the rich people in Manila.

Colegio de Jesus Maria was a Catholic convent school established by the members of the Dominican Order. It was located in a beautiful neighborhood and well kept. Our neat classroom seemed to be a good place for learning where I could thrive and build self-confidence.

The nuns were our teachers, and I learned a lot from them. I learned to respect those in authority but also to always question and analyze. Most of the students were from rich families. They were nice and friendly, and I felt I was with friends who truly understood me. I felt safe with them, and this enabled me to learn and explore freely.

The classroom was well organized and quiet. Everything was conducive to the learning I did. I studied so well that I gained the attention of my teachers.

Because this was a Catholic school, we prayed all the time. At noon, before lunch, we prayed in the classroom, and we went to the chapel daily for Mass. The sisters were very strict when it came to going to the chapel. There was no talking, we had to keep our heads bowed on the way to chapel, and we needed to wear a veil. At twelve years old, I could not understand why these practices were necessary, but I complied.

One day, feeling carefree and playful, I forgot to bring my veil. This one act of forgetfulness did not go unnoticed by one of the nuns. "Thelma Garcia, where is your veil?" she asked furiously. I did not understand then that the veil is an external sign of a woman's internal desire to humble herself before God, truly present in the Blessed Sacrament.

"Sorry, Sister. I forgot to put it inside my bag today," I said softly.

She was outraged by my answer. She frowned, her lower lip quivered, and her face turned red. She took my hand and hauled me off to the lobby of the school and said, "Thelma Rivera Garcia, you will be punished so that you won't forget your veil ever again. Do you hear me?" She roared as if to let everyone in the whole school hear. I did not know what to say. I was scared to death and embarrassed. Sweat beaded my forehead. I tried to hold back my tears as I furtively glanced at the students passing by, staring at me with wide eyes. The nun continued to pull me near the stairs in the lobby where everybody could see me. "Kneel until I tell you to get up," she ordered. "Maybe you will remember to bring your veil next time." Needless to say, I went home that day with a sad face.

This embarrassing incident did not happen only once. I got used to kneeling near the staircase. But every time the senior students who knew me saw me kneeling, they gave me imported chocolates! Which I enjoyed! Soon, I found that the concrete floor was not so bad, and the embarrassment was a small price to pay. After all, those chocolates were a very expensive treat.

I hoped to finish my four-year high school experience on that campus until my mother discovered that some boys were beginning to notice I was developing a gentle, charming personality. Maggie told my mother about the boys who always waited for us every day after school and tried to be friends with me. Afraid that these boys would distract me from my studies, my mother decided to transfer me to another school in Manila. I had no say in the matter.

"Next year, you will be going to another school so you will no longer be distracted by these boys," my mother said. "School is very important for your future."

I bowed my head and whispered to myself, "I wish I could say I could ignore the boys here — that I won't even look at them. I want to stay in my school. I do not like myself being so submissive. I cannot even say no."

The family was then and is now the most important social group in Filipino culture. Close-knit family ties are a large part of Filipino identity. Harmony within the family, respect for elders, fulfilling family duties and expectations, and deferring to the decisions of parents are thought to be very important values to instill in children. Filipino families place great importance on honor, dignity, and decency, and one family member's behavior and achievements reflect on the family as a whole and can bring about family pride or shame. So, Filipino children are expected to obey their parents and sacrifice their own interests for the good of the whole family. This implicit expectation is based on the idea of *utang na loob*, or lifelong debt toward their parents for raising them.

That kind of rearing must have been responsible for my shyness and lack of self-confidence. I always did what my parents desired. I never questioned their rules as those expectations were grounded in my consciousness the day I was born. I was never punished as a child because I was obedient to my parents and elders. I was a good child, very conforming, playful but afraid. I became an underwater spirit, not the bold sun in the sky. I was the Pisces in the cool shallows of the ocean, never the predator that chased from above. I became the wind-bell at Eastertide, never the cloudburst that brings all kinds of wicked confusion. I thought to myself that maybe someday if my parents gave me a chance, I would become the warmth, the love, and the laughter. Yes, maybe someday, when my heart lights the way to a good place, this shy girl could become a champion. Yes, maybe someday.

When we came to Manila after the war, a new life came as well, like an ocean melody rolling over weightless ripples but kissing them with a coolness that brought more vigilance. In that new life, I sought only the brilliant rays in the sky so freely given and nothing more. But that life didn't unfold as a gift with a lovely ribbon and the assurance of contentment. Instead, it paved the way to new fears and for a time became a life journey with such bitterness that it would take a bold heart to grasp it and a valiant step to travel it.

I needed to trust that this splash of peril held great possibilities as I reached for the distant horizon of peace.

I was lost in thought when I heard my mother say, "Are you okay? You seem so sad."

I looked at my mother and softly answered, "I will miss my other school and my classmates."

"What about the boys there?" my mother asked. I did not answer, and she seemed to understand and walked away, leaving me to my solitude. She did not notice how fearful I was. Yes, I was afraid to go to my new school. Fear of the unknown enveloped my whole being. *Would I find new friends? What will the teachers be like? Are there bullies there?* Terror seized me as I sat in my room. I could not see myself in the new school they chose for me. Rumor had it that many gang members terrorized the students every day. I felt sad and terrified thinking about my new school. I could not get up even to eat. I felt lonely, too, and angry — angry because I could not say no. I actually thought the strict nuns were far better than what I would be facing. It is true what they say: You cannot appreciate something until you lose it.

My parents enrolled me at José Abad Santos High School in the Binondo area of Manila, within walking distance of my mother's place of business. "That way," she said, "I can watch you and pick you up from school." The school was named after the fifth chief justice of the Supreme Court of the Philippines. During World War II, when government leaders had fled to the United States in exile, he briefly served as president and commander-in-chief of the armed forces on behalf of President Manuel Quezon. About two months later, on May 2, 1942, Japanese forces executed him for refusing to cooperate with them during their occupation of the country. He refused to be blindfolded as he faced death, saying to his son, "Do not cry, Pepito. Show these people that you are brave. It is an honor to die for one's country. Not everybody has that chance." I thought about what he said as I got ready for school as I was full of trepidation.

On that morning, the clouds had diffused the daylight to a gentle sweetness. They moved much like the ocean, revealing the blue amid the whitish dove-gray, a medley of silver that rippled outward to adorn the sky. The day could bring rain or sunshine. I was hoping for both, for a chance of a rainbow.

I was in a meditative state of mind when I heard my inay say, "Thel, are you ready? Make sure you eat breakfast. Soon I will take you to your new school."

"*Opo*, Inay. I will be ready soon," I answered, using the word for "yes" that Filipino children say to show respect.

I came out of my room pretending to be excited. My grin widened so that even my mother started to smile. I smiled as if I were bursting with happiness. It was then that I realized I could turn my fear, sadness, and terror into wisdom.

My mother walked with me to school that day. It was a long walk, but it did not bother me. I enjoyed looking at all the shops along the way, and there were so many things going on. The street was crowded with people shopping, talking with one another. This day that began as a monochrome was now full of color. I felt a sudden rising up of energy, a joy, coming from that crowd of people. I could see the colors in that crowd. A rainbow of people arced its way through the blacktopped street. I saw the rainbow I was hoping for.

The walls along this street, though, were covered with graffiti, mostly the names of gangs. They were colorful but gave me goosebumps. *Who are they? What are they?* I wondered. This place was very different from my other school. At Colegio de Jesus Maria, people were nice, the roads were perfect, and the walk on my way to school was through a park that was peaceful, solemn, and protected from vandalism.

I continued to walk, aware of my anxiety, which became a kind of background noise, like the traffic on some unseen road. I thought, *I think this feeling is normal and natural. It is, after all, part of how we keep ourselves safe and well.* I thought, though, that I had to be careful because this anxiety could affect both my brain and my body. "I am brave. All will be well," I muttered to myself. Unfortunately, my body and my brain were unconvinced, and I started to have scary and uncomfortable thoughts. My heart was racing, I started to feel discomfort in my chest, and my jaw tightened. I was no longer smiling about my rainbow. Anxiety is like being hooked up to an electric cattle fence: The voltage is not enough to kill but sufficient to make things uncomfortable.

My new school was huge, ten times larger than my other school, and had so many students! The sophomore class was so big that students were divided into six sections, with thirty students in a class. We were divided according to our study habits and intellectual abilities. I was in Section 1, a better section than all of the others. The only drawback was that I had to work harder to keep my place there.

"Welcome to José Abad Santos High School, Thelma," said the principal of the school as he greeted me on this day of orientation. "I hope you have a great experience in this school. Wait for me, and I will take you on a tour of the school and introduce you to your homeroom teacher."

"What is a homeroom teacher, sir?" I politely asked. "I did not have one at my other school. We were only thirty students in my freshman class."

"Oh, don't worry. I will take you to her so she can explain it to you."

My homeroom teacher was beautiful. She was about forty years old, of medium height, and had a fair complexion. Her smile was inviting and her voice soothing yet confident. She commanded respect but was also accommodating.

Like all homeroom teachers, she made sure we had all the books and any other materials we would need for our studies. She also kept track of who was present and who was absent and found ways to get to know us better in order to help us with any problems we might have. She was also responsible for our safety and helping us adjust to the school.

"Thelma, please make sure to let me know if anything is bothering you so I can help you in your studies and your transition to our school," she said in a very welcoming voice. "Please make sure you use the buddy system whenever you are out of the classroom so you can be safe, especially going to the restroom," she added. "Also, be very careful in dealing with gangs in the school. Please let me know if any of them are bothering you."

I knew then that my homeroom teacher had a good heart. "Yes, ma'am," I answered softly. I felt my mind come alive. I felt that learning would come easy.

On the way home, I glanced at the wall of graffiti that had so frightened me and said to myself, "Tomorrow I will meet my classmates, and I will be at ease."

After the blackness of the night, Earth's star rose on the horizon and spread her gold in every direction. It came in the way that natural forces do, needing no invitation yet feeling an utmost welcome. This is her gift, bold and free, for anyone who cares to open their eyes in the dawn and watch the world awaken. Like me. I was so excited to meet my new classmates. I dressed up, choosing the best school dress I could find. I smiled as I heard Maggie, my yaya, call, "Thel, breakfast is ready. Come so you won't be late for school!"

"Okay, thank you. I will be there in a minute." I glanced at the mirror and flew down the stairs.

"You look beautiful," Maggie said.

"Thank you so much," I answered excitedly.

"Your black hair is beautiful hanging down to your shoulders now. You gained a little bit of weight, and your fair complexion definitely complements your big, brown eyes." I was eating as fast as I could while listening to my *yaya* speak. "You better watch out; the boys will notice you. That means trouble, remember?" I just smiled and hurriedly left for school.

The bell had not yet rung when I arrived at school, so I had time to observe the other students, who all looked clean and well-dressed for school. They seemed happy chatting with one another, finding friends, laughing, giggling, and having a great time. "What a happy bunch," I said to myself. "I wonder if I will meet a friend today." My eyes caught sight of a group of students near the school gate not too far from where I stood. They looked different. Some of them had tattoos on their arms and looked a little older than me, maybe sixteen to eighteen years old. They dressed as if they belonged to a gang, not a school. They looked tough. They looked to me like they were trying to find their first victim of the day. This was my first encounter with bullies, so I was worried and scared. I tried to ignore them, but the one who seemed to be the leader of the gang waved at me, so I hesitantly, and with trepidation, waved back. He looked older than the rest of the group. He wore a red bandana, dirty jeans, and a wrinkled top.

The tattoo on his arm looked like a snake. I wondered what that represented in his life. Were his emotions engraved in that tattoo? So much aggression and so much pain. I thought to myself, *Is that your way out? Is that how you hide your pain? Don't you know that your hiding will become an endless marathon of bleeding knees? Don't you know that living with an incomplete soul is a form of death? Would you rather be a humane human than a zombie needing to bite somebody to live?*

Suddenly, I heard the bell ring, breaking through my thoughts, so I went to line up for class and met my first classmate.

"Hi. My name is Ignacio. I am the class representative. Welcome to the class," Ignacio said with a big smile.

"Hi. I'm Thelma. This is my first day here."

I was thrilled to have met some good friends that day. I met Elizabeth, Mary, another girl named Thelma, and some boys besides Ignacio. I told my new friends about the boys I had seen earlier near the school gate.

Thelma said, "Be careful around them. They belong to a gang, and they bully students here. Do you know anything about bullies?"

"No. I have not encountered anybody like that in my life," I said. I told her the only thing I knew about bullies was what I had read in books. I told her that I understood that bullying had become very common in schools and that bullies abused other students by assaulting them either verbally or physically to make themselves look powerful. I told her that I had read that if someone was confident and didn't react to a bully's threats, the bully would most likely leave them alone. I told her that other than that, the idea of bullies was very new to me.

"Okay," Thelma said. "Just be careful."

That day, I also learned the reason for the buddy system that my homeroom teacher mentioned to me. The year before, a freshman girl had been stabbed several times in the bathroom for unknown reasons. From then on, no one was ever to go anywhere in school alone.

Several days later, I was walking to my class and joyfully looking forward to making plans for a school party. I was feeling hopeful. A beautiful morning tells us in various ways that every day of our lives is a new beginning. This morning had delivered glittering rays of sun in hues of shiny silver and gold. I embraced the day and wondered what treasures it would bring.

Suddenly, out of the blue, the head of the bullying gang came up to me and introduced himself. "Hi, I'm Jay," he said. "Who are you?"

I was so surprised, but I managed to smile and say, "Hi, I'm Thelma."

"I know you. Thank you for stopping and talking to me," he said. "Not everybody talks to me. I guess they are scared."

"Okay. Bye," I said. I smiled and continued to walk to the classroom.

"Okay," he replied. "See you later."

My friend Elizabeth saw him leave and said, "Thelma, be careful. Tell the teacher if he's bothering you. Okay?"

"Okay," I said.

The following day at recess, Jay came and gave me an ice cream sandwich. I could not refuse it out of fear that he would explode in anger, so I accepted it. I talked to him as a friend and showed him that I respected him. He seemed relaxed with me. I could not eat the ice cream he gave me because I thought I might be allergic to some of its ingredients. At the same time, I could not refuse it because I thought he might be offended. I put it on my desk. Needless to say, it started melting, and the teacher noticed.

"Thelma, something is leaking from your desk. What is it?" she asked.

"It's ice cream, ma'am." I explained the situation with Jay.

She seemed to understand my dilemma and said, "Okay. Here is a plastic bag. Next time you come to school, bring a plastic bag so this type of thing won't happen again. By the way, Thelma, I like the way you handled the bully with respect. Sometimes that is all they need."

"Thank you, ma'am," I said gratefully. After that, every time Jay would give me an ice cream sandwich, I had a plastic bag ready.

Jay became a friend of mine until he moved to another district. I learned so much about how to deal with a bully from him. He often watched me as I walked home so that I would be safe on the street. He became my protector, my defender, and a friend in need. I learned from him the meaning and power of respect — that respect means that you accept somebody for who they are even when they have different ideas from yours.

I loved the years I spent at José Abad Santos High School. It was a wonderful period in my life and a golden time of learning. Besides what I learned in my classes, I also learned dedication, hard work, and self-actualization. I am most grateful for the good friends I had. The joys and sorrows we shared helped us build a great foundation for life. To me, friendship feels like the water that flows between open fingers in a summer stream and warm woolens and the hearth when wintry winds blow. In times of danger, it becomes a sword and a shield. The thought of going to high school had terrified me at first, but with time, I was able to appreciate and treasure everything about it. I experienced the worst and the best in high school; it's all part of growing up. I lost one of my good friends in high school. His death was painful, but with the help of friends and school officials, I came to understand the real meaning of life and death. High school days can be the most formative period in our lives. The concept of life becomes clear here, and I got a glimpse of how the real world works.

CHAPTER 7

Ate Lunding Gets Sick

Having a sister is like having a best friend
you can't get rid of.
You know whatever you do,
they'll still be there.

— *Amy Li*

MY ATE LUNDING BECAME MY eldest sibling when my brother Ka Asias died. Ate Lunding and I are sisters by blood and in our souls. She and I are the sun, moon, and stars to one another.

Ate Lunding looks to be a blend of Spanish and Filipino descent. She is tiny and beautiful, and her face shines with innocent eyes and a huge smile. She is incredibly outgoing and happy. "Bubbly" is the word that comes to mind when describing her. "Happiness is the only way to survive," she would tell me.

Ate Lunding is also the most determined and organized person I know and can sit for hours poring over papers in her work as a dental assistant responsible for billing and paperwork. Although my sister is constantly busy, she knows how to find balance in her life, and the stress of everyday living doesn't seem to bother her. When I was little, she came home late one night from a dance party and dragged me out of bed. When I moaned, "What are you doing?" she said, "Let's dance! Dance!" A confident person! She turned on the music, grabbed me, and we danced until we heard my mother's voice: "Hey, you two! Turn the music off and go to bed!" We both giggled happily and complied.

Ate Lunding married Bonifacio Bitonio, a lovely man introduced to Ate Lunding by my Ate Remy, who was working as a nurse in Guam. Bonifacio worked as a construction worker in Guam. Ate Lunding and Bonifacio fell in love and got married when I was about seven years old. I was their flower girl. I felt so proud that day and so happy for her. They lived in the downstairs unit in our house in San Juan, Rizal. We lived upstairs. My sister stayed close to us even though she was married and had children, staying true to one of the many treasured Filipino traditions.

Filipinos are known to have close family ties. We place the family before anything else. It seems that in most other countries, when a young person turns eighteen, they leave home to find a place of their own away from family. In the Philippines, however, they will stay with the family through the years.

This is just one of the many traditions in the Philippines that I hold dear. Another that I think is important to mention is that we are taught to be respectful and courteous. One traditional way to show elders our respect is to use the gesture *mano po*, which literally means "your hand, please." The one wishing to show respect places the back of the elder's hand lightly on his forehead and addresses the elder, if a sibling, as *Kuya* or *Ate*.

Another tradition of the people of the Philippines that I think is important is placing God at the center of family life. Also, in changing and challenging situations, we choose to be flexible and to cooperate in order to be helpful. We do not let our family go through crises alone; instead, we help them. We are also very hospitable people. When we expect visitors, we make a lot of preparations to feed and entertain them and provide good accommodations so that they can feel at home. Also, we show our gratitude when someone helps us, and we try our best to repay them. And through good times and bad, Filipinos always find a way to smile and be happy. I am proud to have these distinguished traditions, and I hope they continue for years to come.

True to our Filipino tradition, my parents made sure that when Ate Lunding got married, she would be near us. Her place downstairs was self-contained with three bedrooms, a living room, a dining room, a kitchen, and two bathrooms. This was enough for her family, which included her husband and their four children: Tessie, Alice, Edgar, and Jun. I liked the way she decorated her home. It was a kaleidoscope of memories. The walls were decorated with family photographs, each one bringing to mind sweet memories.

Outside was a beautiful garden. I loved the way the garden gave us a place to meditate. We made sure to plant the kind of vegetation that helped Mother Nature. We had fruit-bearing trees — star apples, Spanish plums, mangoes, and many more. We even had chickens, a turkey, and a baby pig. A big backyard and a playground for my sister's kids were next to this garden.

We enjoyed every moment in the garden. We had all our family get-togethers there. We even enjoyed it when it rained. The garden was always a bright hue. The rain was not water but fluid magic that cleansed our universe to show what was there all along — nature in her humble brightness and luster. The goblet became gold, the grass grew like the shadow of every dream's pasture, so beautiful to see, and the soil resurrected. After the patter of the rain came the bursting forth of birdsong, the birds' hearts rejoicing in its coming.

This was our family home and our family garden. Our house was a house of peace that sheltered our family with a great foundation of love: perfectly sound, set to stand for all generations to come.

I came home to this house from my dorm at the University of the Philippines in June 1960. My liberal arts studies had come to an end, and I was ready to apply for a nursing internship for the coming year. I was so excited to come home and take a break from my hectic school schedule. "Thank God, it's done and over," I muttered to myself. "Finally, I can just take it easy."

That night seemed to be special. The stars filled the sky like snowflakes in the night — still, like a portrait. "What a beautiful sight," I said as I slowly drifted into slumber. I was halfway to wakefulness, halfway to my dreams of the night as they fashioned into new dreams, when I heard Maggie, my yaya, banging my bedroom door and shouting, "Thel, wake up! Ate Lunding is very sick!"

"What?" I slowly answered as I jumped from my bed to open the door. "What happened?" I asked and ran down to my sister's home on the first floor.

"I don't know, but she is really sick," Maggie replied.

I hurriedly opened my sister's bedroom door. I froze at the sight. My thoughts spun out of control with fear. I felt like I was having a heart attack. My body trembled; my eyes flooded with tears. *Please help me, my God,* I silently prayed. The sight of my sister vomiting blood scared me to death, but I knew I needed to act fast.

I brought a bucket for her to vomit in. Big clots of blood came from her mouth, which I wiped with a towel. There was so much bloody vomit that it splashed onto my clothes, and soon I was covered with blood too. I called Maggie and told her to go to our neighbor. "I am taking Ate to the hospital," I said. "Please call my mother to tell her to meet us at San Lazaro Hospital in Manila and to make it fast."

Our neighbors took us to the hospital in their jeep. On the way, I glanced at my sister, whose beautiful face was once so full of life, whose spirit was always so "bubbly," who now looked as pale as a white sheet. She was trembling with fear, unable to breathe, her body as cold as ice. She whispered to me, "Thelma, please take care of the children."

I looked at her helplessly but was able to utter, "Yes, Ate. Don't worry. They are okay. I left instructions to the helper to make sure the children are safe." She closed her eyes but held my hand tightly.

San Lazaro Hospital specialized in treating contagious diseases like tuberculosis, which turned out to be my sister's diagnosis. When we got to the hospital, a stretcher was ready for her, and a nurse gave me a gown to change into so I could get out of my bloody clothes and wash the blood from my body. My mother was already there and waiting for us. I was so glad she got there in time with money so my sister could be treated.

With a diagnosis of tuberculosis, my sister was put in isolation, and nobody could visit her until she got better. I felt sad for her. She was in isolation for a long time. Family and friends could not visit, but she did write to me:

"I had so many panicky moments at first, yet over time they grew further apart and disappeared. I found a new joy in nature, little things, like waiting for birdsong and the simple pleasure of a burst of sunlight on my skin. It is very taxing, yet I have become indestructible. I can now say I am better at being alone. Thelma, in isolation, I feel at times as if seized by fire, yet after this, I know I will come out strong, so I keep on praying that all will be well in time. Thel, please keep the best version of yourself, and please take care of the children. I love them so much. Please take care and be healthy, and I love you forever."

Your loving sister,

Ate Lunding

My sister finally got well, and I took care of her when she got home. Our life went back to normal with high hopes for good health and love.

CHAPTER 8

Illness Puts College on Hold

Knowledge is a commodity to be shared.
For knowledge to pay dividends,
it should not remain the monopoly
of the selected few.

— *Moutasem Algharati*

SUMMER WAS GONE. IT IS funny how those warm days seemed so free, unlocked as if the sparkle of summer itself was an entrée into a dream world of fantasy.

It was a perfect day for me to go to apply for a nursing internship. The weather was nice, as if it were cooperating with me on this important day. I loved the day. I loved the random sounds that came as I rested my thoughts in the clouds that were my dreams — stray ideas that indulged my mind. In the sunshine, every color came into focus beneath a picture-perfect blue sky to enhance the world it praised.

The dean conducting the interview checked my grades but first had my chest X-rayed when he learned my sister had been sick with tuberculosis a few months before. I went home hopeful because I did not have any symptoms.

When I got home, Ate Lunding was waiting for me. "How did it go?" she inquired.

"I don't know yet," I answered. "I had a chest X-ray done, and I am now waiting for the results. Hope all is well."

I learned that day to wait with patience. I tried very hard to be emotionally mature as I anticipated the results, hoping that patience now would eventually lead to greater happiness later. It was not easy.

I tried to do the things I usually do, but I was worried. So many questions ran through my mind. *What if they saw something in my X-ray? Would I have to stop attending school? Who would take care of me? What would happen to my life? My dreams? Would they put me in isolation like my sister?* I did my very best to enjoy myself while waiting for the results, but I became apprehensive. There was a feeling in my gut that said the results would show a problem, but my heart said I would be fine. What are we if we don't find the courage to fight for ourselves? To be this afraid of something or someone seemed to me to be rubbish, really. So, I chose to be brave instead of being a puppet of fear.

Then one day, I got a letter that said I had a spot on my lungs and my application had been turned down. I had to be healthy before they could accept me. It meant I had to put my plans for an internship on hold. Anxiety overcame me, and I felt sick to my stomach. My mother saw my troubled face and asked me why I looked so terrified.

"I won't be able to continue school. I have a spot on my lungs," I tearfully answered. "What am I to do?"

My mother, bless her beautiful heart, held me in her arms and said, "Don't worry. All will be fine. I will call our family doctor, and we will see what he says. For now, I want you to dry your tears and have some fresh fruit for a snack. All will be fine." She continued to reassure me. "Do not worry about school. I promise that you will be back to school as soon as you are well." I was so glad my mother was so loving and understanding, and I felt better. Her tranquil presence calmed my heart and soul.

My mother was always the sustaining force in our family, a strong, loving, and very powerful influence in my life. She was my first best friend. My world was sometimes a velvety night and sometimes inky black, but her presence was the light that grew inside my soul and shone through my eyes. She was the best mother and a great mentor to all her children. She always addressed our emotional needs before speaking logically about the situation. She was a reliable and safe place to anchor our hearts, so we always felt that our souls were nurtured and valued. She was the strongest person I ever met and the softest, and the one who realized that true power is lifting others up. The real power of love for her was elevating and educating. I was blessed to have had such a wonderful mother who supported and loved us the way she did.

True to her word, my mother made an appointment for the doctor to see me the following day. Dr. Diaz entered the room. In any other clothes, he would have appeared too young for the job. He checked the charts to see what was wrong with me. We chatted about school. He was excited to find out I wanted to be a nurse. His speech was peppered with humor though it was never inappropriate. He listened to me and asked all the right questions to get the information he needed. He ordered some tests and held off making a diagnosis before the lab results were done. He reassured me that he would call me and give me any information that I wanted when the lab results came back.

The lab results showed I was positive for tuberculosis, but the infection was not serious enough to warrant hospitalization. I felt so relieved as I didn't want to be hospitalized as my sister had been. I had learned a lot about this disease by reading about it and asking questions, and I wanted to learn more about it so I could be cured fast. I wanted to go back to school as soon as possible.

I learned that tuberculosis is a contagious infection caused by a bacterium called Mycobacterium tuberculosis. It is common in the lungs but can affect other parts of the body as well and usually causes localized symptoms in the area it has infected. It is a major health problem worldwide. Although it is caused by bacteria, it is resistant to many antibiotics and is often difficult to treat. Some patients need to have multiple antibiotics administered for many months.

Several factors contribute to acquiring TB: (1) Visiting a high-risk location. TB can occur anywhere, but a few locations have very high rates, including Africa and parts of Asia. (2) Transmission from person to person.

This is what happened to me when I took care of my sister at home. It is also spread through the air by coughing, sneezing, spitting, or speaking. Sharing food, drinks, or utensils with people infected with TB can also put someone at high risk. Drug addicts and homeless people are at high risk of becoming infected. (3) Receiving an organ transplant. This can lower one's resistance to the disease.

I also learned that it weakens the immune system and can be deadly, but a person can also be infected by the bacteria and not even get the disease. Most importantly, TB is preventable by early detection, vaccination, and proper treatment.

I learned so much about the disease that I didn't fear it as before. I made small changes and made them slowly rather than all at once. One small change at a time makes the result last longer. I started to exercise and developed healthy eating habits, eating more vegetables and other good food. I began to take precautions like washing my hands and sanitizing utensils. Most important is that I developed the habit of thankfulness every day. I discovered that gratitude is a powerful catalyst for happiness, and happiness leads to a healthy life. Every day, I become healthier and more aware of all the necessary tools to stay healthy. I hope that people gain more awareness about TB, its treatment, and its prevention.

CHAPTER 9

Get Ready, Here I Come!

*If you feel like there is something out there
that you are supposed to be doing,
if you have passion for it, then stop wishing
and just do it.*

— *Wanda Sykes*

GROWING UP IS SOMETHING WE all have to face. The process of changing from a naive child into a mature adult is shaped by the influential people in our lives. It is not an easy process, but with proper support and guidance, we are able to develop a healthy sense of responsibility and independence. We evolve from being a child who is told what to do into an adult who makes their own decisions. Becoming independent was a frightening experience for me.

I believe the bond between siblings is the most enduring bond that any of us can experience and that the quality of that bond determines the quality of all of our relationships. This bond is not supposed to be as demanding or as critical as that of the bond with our parents, but it was different for me.

I grew up alongside my three brothers — Kuya Lando, Alfredo, and Timoteo. When my brother Alfredo was fourteen years old, he was a typical teenager. He had tantalizing, big, brown eyes, liked to dress well, was very smart, and had a great personality. He loved to play chess and was very good at it. He was a good brother to me. He would tell me the names of all the boys in the neighborhood who liked me and would carry their letters to me. "Ate Tem, you sure are liked by the following boys," he would whisper so my parents wouldn't hear. He would tell me who really cared for me.

The youngest of all my brothers was Timoteo. We called him "Sonny" because he was the last son. He was very intelligent, happy, creative, and handsome, with nice, brown eyes. His features were Spanish-looking, like my itay. He liked to sing and was very playful. He was my dad's favorite son.

Kuya Lando was a handsome young man with fair skin and brown eyes. He was very intelligent and had a very good command of the English language. He somehow managed to memorize an English dictionary. He was a law student.

My sister Ate Luz had gone to Guam to work as a nurse alongside my Ate Remy at Guam Memorial Hospital. As a result, my life involved running the streets of Manila and San Juan, Rizal, with three rambunctious but very protective brothers. It was a precautious, sometimes dubious bubble of security but one that gave me the opportunity to continue to be that eleven-year-old little girl far into adulthood.

I often accepted potential failure because my Kuya Lando, the handsome student of law, was always pushing me, toughening me up, quizzing me, interrogating me like a witness in court. I became his guinea pig witness in the courtroom in our house.

"So, Tem," he would say, "what do you think of this?" We would be on the car-choked street at our house in Manila. He would not stop until I gave a decent answer to his question. One muggy day, he asked me, "Why does this movie have a better plot than this other one?"

"I don't know; I don't like that movie," I replied, trying to get out of the interrogation, but he wouldn't stop until I gave a better answer.

Those interrogations continued every day. "Tem, who do you think is smarter, Filipinos or Chinese?"

"I don't know. I think both of them are smart."

"Hmm," he would grunt with a slow-burning cigarette in his mouth.

When he felt generous, he would let the conversation go but always asked the same question in a different way later on. I remember my brother doing that every day. I felt like I was being bullied by my own brother. At times, I wondered if I would have been better off being bullied at school than at home. That way, I could have told someone — a teacher or a friend. But at home, there was no escape. Every day, my tormentor was there waiting for me in the court of interrogation. Never did I know that my brother loved me most. He was trying to toughen me up with his questions, trying to help me think of a solution rather than giving up. He helped me become a powerful woman with those days of interrogation and forced thinking.

Our unspoken roles were also roadmaps with boundaries and guideposts. When I was young, I never understood the big picture. I was the quintessential baby girl, spoiled but protected by my brothers' constant watching and Lando's questioning. My brothers allowed me to learn about games within games, playing and acting them out on the street, and I became strong. And for that, I am forever indebted to them. Fear used to come to me in crashing waves, like those on a winter beach, without any warmth. It used to come as a chill that went to the core of who I was and snarled so I would cower.

With my brother Lando's help and guidance, I learned how to swim through that ice and live in the salty water with my courage as a furnace. He helped me be brave by constantly training my mind to think and search for the answers to his questions. He helped me develop the strength to conquer fear and accept pain and humiliation as lessons I needed to master. I chose to walk through hell to find my heaven. I chose to not just walk but to run. That's being brave, and I am proud of my choice.

I am a petite woman, but I have proved my worth physically and emotionally. I felt proud and blessed to have had my brothers. I became a woman when I made the choice to not be afraid every time I applied to a nursing school and was rejected. I was able to think clearly and developed powerful thoughts that kept me from sliding into fear. I continued to apply to nursing schools, but I decided that whatever happened to my application, I would keep my faith. I also developed a plan just in case I failed to get an internship.

I had other courses to take. I talked to my parents about changing my major, and they were okay with the possibilities I presented to them. I began to look into other courses at other universities. I had opened my mind to the heavens above to lead me to the right path. I kept myself healthy, and I got ready for greater possibilities that would come into my life.

I did all in my power to get into a nursing school but with no luck despite my good grades. Most of the colleges I looked at wanted students to be at least five feet tall. Unfortunately, I was only four foot, eleven. I was told that height was important because we had to lift patients and care for people of all different sizes. Still, I did not give up. I exercised to try to add some inches to my height. I exercised to be healthy.

This life was really tough for me. Things don't always work out well, but I needed to be brave and keep trying as I believed that the best was yet to come. In the process of finding myself, I discovered the parts of me that had been hidden, and I developed self-control, greater creativity, and new skills, such as logical thinking skills. I practiced being present with myself in every moment, becoming aware of my feelings, and being willing to analyze my feelings and my motivations from many perspectives.

Finally, I am there. Finally, I believe in myself. Finally, I am my true self, the person I was born to be, one who seeks and gives love. I feel healed in a way and can't recall ever feeling sick. It's healthy. I wish everyone could find it.

For a while, I thought the battle was me versus me, but in that struggle to become my better self, the battle became a collaboration: me *and* me. I was on the road to self-respect and enlightenment, the road to becoming my hero self. I have become brave, alive, healthy, loving with all my heart. I have stayed on the road of empathy and compassion, love and fraternity, with a determination that will accept death over failure. I have the spirit of a child but the nobility of a true warrior, always protective and kind. Now I can dream wild in starlight. I finally realize that I am good at my core, and I know my self-worth. A solid sense of confidence expands from within. Passion becomes my rocket fuel and, combined with determination, full liftoff occurs, and I am ready.

CHAPTER 10

Thank You, I'm Accepted!

*With your entire focus on your goal, you will
reach levels of achievement
that you never thought possible.*

— *Catherine Pulsifer*

THE SUN ROSE AS A canopy of gold, bright amid the blue, bidding the stars to take their rest. As the darkness surrendered, every color changed from charcoal-tinged to vibrant. There are days that I wonder what we give in return for such a gift of divine magic. Perhaps it is our love. Perhaps we radiate it into space. Perhaps that is our connection to creation beyond our world, our reality. Today, the sky was a billion pure rays of light. It was as if night and day had become one beautiful moment. The dawn had come.

I was starting out early to go to the Philippine Women's University (PWU) on Taft Avenue. The news said that a new dean had come to start a new nursing curriculum. I had hoped that this university would be a good place to meet new friends and form new relationships, a good space to become a young-adult version of myself, a good place to expand the horizon of what I had previously believed possible.

PWU was established as the Philippine Women's College in 1919, during the American colonial era, by a group of Filipino women: Clara Aragon, Concepcion Aragon, Francisca Tirona Benitez, Paz Marquez Benitez, Carolina Ocampo, Palma Mercedes Rivera, and Soccoro Marquez. It was the first university for women in Asia founded by Asians.

According to the PWU School of Nursing Facebook page, PWU began offering nursing education in 1950 for graduates of hospital schools of nursing. "In response to a very inspiring clamor to offer a basic nursing program, a feasibility study on 'The Projected College of Nursing in the Philippine Women's University' by Anastacia Giron Tupaz was tested out." In 1960, the PWU College of Nursing came into being and offered a five-year, integrated curriculum leading to a Bachelor of Science in Nursing degree. The aim of the College of Nursing was, and still is, "to prepare professional nurses for service in a changing society." It is the first school in the history of nursing education that includes a practicum in its curriculum.

I had submitted to PWU School of Nursing all the documentation required and had passed the entrance examination, and now I needed to meet with the dean for an interview.

As I dressed to get ready for the big day, I felt an explosion of excitement. All of my ideas about the possibilities that lay ahead felt like a buzz of electricity, a calling card of adventure to paths awaiting my feet. I did not know what was ahead, but whatever it was would be a great challenge. There could be tears again like before, but this was my adventure to take, and so I smiled.

I heard my brother call, "Tem, are you ready? I took a day off so I can take you to the university."

"Hmm," I said to myself but answered him excitedly, "Thank you so much. Now I feel better. I will be there shortly."

My brother Kuya Lando, my interrogator, had been a great source of support during my ordeal. He had always been willing to take me anywhere to apply to different universities. And for that, I was grateful. He stood by me every step of the way, whether it was a good day or bad, although he never stopped in his efforts to encourage me to develop my reasoning abilities.

"Are you ready to face the dean of the university?" my brother asked.

"I think so," I softly answered.

"Tem, do not say, 'I think so,' but instead say, 'Yes I am ready,'" he said in a firm voice. "That way, your brain and your inner mind will be in harmony, and you will *feel* ready."

After a short pause, he again asked, "Are you ready for the big interview with the dean of the university?" This time, his voice was loud, like a rumble of roaring thunder.

I stood there and, with all my strength, I shouted, "Yes! Yes! I am ready to face the dean today!" and danced like a chicken after it lays an egg.

He happily hugged me, lifted me up a little, and said excitedly, "Yay! That's my girl! Now let's do this!"

I knew he really wanted me to be admitted because he had to take me to all the interviews. Sometimes, the interviewer thought he was the one applying because he always did the talking. I was too shy. Oftentimes, he would say, "Tem, you better open your mouth. These people think I want to be a nurse. You know they always want the handsome ones." I would just laugh. I am grateful for the support of my big brother, and my whole family, in all of my endeavors in life. Ivan Pavlov, a Russian physiologist, said, "Perfect as the wing of a bird may be, it will never enable the bird to fly if unsupported by air." My brother, my family, are my air.

That day, I decided to take a big leap of faith and visit the dean's office by myself. My decision amazed me! I had seen awesome before, but now I *was* awesome! I was joyful! I realized at that moment that even the wind was refreshing, and the rain was cleansing when one felt joy. Every small thing in life is an opportunity to nourish the soul if we let joy in. I decided to live with awe and humbleness, to be present in every moment. I felt the gifts of life filling me to the brim, so much so that my joy overflowed. I found serenity in joy, an essential ingredient of my pilot light. Fear used to envelop my being every time I faced the interview process. The color drained from my face, and I shook with terror. I could not talk. But this day was different. I felt confident with joy on my face.

"Good morning, Miss Garcia. How are you?" the dean said, welcoming me with a smile.

I smiled back and said, "I am good, thank you. How are you, Mrs. Tupaz?"

"I am fine, thank you," she answered gracefully. She looked a bit older than I imagined, but I could see the beauty in her gestures, and her smile showed a genuine concern for her students. She said, "Miss Garcia, your grades are excellent. You can be anything with these grades. Why do you want to be a nurse?"

"Ma'am, I would like to be a nurse because I have an inborn desire to care for people in times of need," I answered. I went on to tell her that I thought helping people overcome the burden of different health conditions and supporting their families through such difficulties was very important. I said I thought the medical field was a dynamic profession, and its different approaches to wellness and health care were capable of improving the quality of life overall. I told her I wanted to be a part of that experience with the great hope that I could get involved with research and the education of the masses.

"Being a nurse will help me develop the ability to handle both saving lives and losing lives, which I see as amazing acts of love," I said. "I am willing to work hard and in different health environments to continue to help people in need. I will do whatever it takes to be an excellent nurse and hopefully become an inspiration to many student nurses who follow me."

I paused and then said sadly, "The only thing is, my height is not good enough for the other schools of nursing. I am only four foot, eleven."

To my surprise, Mrs. Tupaz got up and hugged me and said, "Miss Garcia, our new curriculum does not include that requirement. You have excellent grades and a beautiful mission in taking this course. I bet my life you will be an excellent nurse. Please go to the registrar's office and fill out the necessary papers, and I will see you in class in a month."

My heart leaped with joy! It was the best news I had heard in years. This was one of the happiest moments in my life. Finally, my application was accepted. I was going to college!

I believe that when someone is on a mission with a great desire and absolute commitment, the universe moves in miraculous ways to make it happen. For that, I am truly grateful.

Needless to say, my kuya was very happy about the good news, and he took me to lunch at my favorite restaurant.

CHAPTER 11

My Life and Friends at PWU

*People will forget what you said, people
will forget what you did,
but people will never forget
how you made them feel.*

— *Maya Angelou*

I WOKE UP IN THE early morning when the hues of the world bloomed anew as if each were a tiny flower reborn. The sunlight roused more colors from their sleepy monochrome, and though the road still had the black look of the night, the sky was already more bluish than charcoal.

I put on my white uniform with its maroon lettering. This was my first day of nursing school. This was the day I would become part of the Philippine Women's University community and begin my journey on the path to becoming the fine nurse I wished to be. This was the day I would meet my new family, the one I would spend years learning with. I would meet my new sisters from all walks of life and from different parts of the Philippines. It would truly be a divine pleasure to meet someone new.

I was sure my first day on campus would be memorable. My dream was becoming a reality. My heart soared thinking about this new place, this new life, this new lifestyle, a totally new world for me after being sick and having to stay home for a year

One of the most impressive traditions of this university was its welcome party for new students. We gathered in the foyer of the university, a spacious area perfect for us to come together and meet new friends. The president welcomed us as if we were family and gave us very useful guidance for being successful in university life. Afterward, we were served refreshments and had a great time giggling with newfound friends, my future family.

We did attend some classes that first day, mainly to get our schedules and learn the rules and regulations. It was a joyful day of colorful events. The students were very friendly, including Minerva, a very petite lady with big, brown eyes, black hair that reached to her shoulders, and a slightly dark complexion. Her oval face wore a beautiful smile that seemed to brighten the day.

"Hi," she said with grace as she shook my hand to introduce herself. "I am Minerva. I am from Parañaque, Rizal."

"Hello. My name is Thelma, but you can call me Thel. I am from San Juan, Rizal," I answered excitedly and for some reason mentioned that I had a pharmacology class at 1 p.m.

"Wow, I have that class too," Minerva said. "Let's meet up at the cafeteria, and then we can go to the class together."

"Okay," I said.

The days that followed were mostly about meeting professors and new friends. I met so many beautiful people and found so many good friends at PWU — Zeny, Lai, Angie, Meng Joy, Diane, Letty, and the whole Nursing Council, which includes all the nursing students in the university. We became one family with one heart. I was truly blessed.

My friends who believe in me make a cradle for my soul. My friends at PWU believed in me. They are the very fabric that keeps me warm, and so I am grateful to the universe and every star above that we made our way together. Our friendship is like the soft colors of nature, the delicate browns of the Earth, and the deep blues of the sky that show us the stars. It's an earthiness that lasts a lifetime.

As I dove into my nursing courses, I discovered that nursing was art, so I was an artist. It required as much devotion to hard preparation as any painting or sculpture. Nursing to me was the finest art. While the painter worked with hard canvases and the sculptor with dead marble, I worked with the living body, the temple of God's spirit.

PWU provided me with all the tools necessary to develop that wonderful art of nursing. As a student working toward a bachelor's degree in nursing, I was prepared for a successful career in the health and wellness industry. I was trained in preventing diseases, promoting health, restoring health, and alleviating suffering. My education also included real-life nursing experience at Rizal Provincial Medical Center, our base hospital, and other hospitals, such as Victoriano Luna Hospital and Veterans Hospital Manila.

Being a student nurse brought many challenges every day, such as trying to complete assignments on time and frantically trying to get a skill signoff for procedures like making beds, giving injections, and cutting a baby's cord in front of the instructor. If a student passed, the instructor signed your signoff sheet. Simply trying to find the energy to iron my uniform after a long shift was a challenge. What made me go on? My friends. They made me realize that these challenges did not compare to the ones many patients encountered daily. I thought of one of my patients who had leukemia. He was young, a student, and had to undergo treatment every day. It broke my heart to see him suffer. I am forever putting my own life into perspective to realize how truly lucky I and many others are to have good health — in body, mind, and spirit.

To get a range of experiences for the best development of our careers, we were required to work in different specialties. Working in pediatrics was especially rewarding for me. It was a joy to meet and care for so many courageous children and their families. I witnessed their remarkable strength and resilience each day. They motivated me to deliver the best care I could; they deserved nothing less. Being a student nurse in pediatrics taught me to care for not only the patient but for the family as well because they were on the journey too. I experienced a wide range of emotions. I felt awkward comforting a crying parent as they watched their child being anesthetized and taken into surgery. I had known them for only a few hours, but I had a role to play as a future nurse — to care for them, softly pat them on the back to reassure them, lend them a shoulder to cry on, and even give them a hug, all without hesitation. I thought that if I couldn't show that level of compassion and empathy, I wasn't fulfilling my role as a human being.

Another course I took my first year focused on nursing care in the community. This included home visits, a very different world from life on the wards. The work was slightly more relaxed compared to the busy pace of a ward, but do not doubt the workload. One baby was born every forty seconds in the Philippines at that time, and each one needed a visiting nurse. I was busy, but I enjoyed this type of health care. Caring for patients with special needs and complex problems was a good learning experience for me. To see the small yet significant impact I was making for these children and their families inspired me and served as a valuable experience for my future practice.

I met many beautiful people in the poor areas of the community. I became more aware of these areas and of the help needed to improve the health and lives of the people there. Most were trying to help themselves despite the poverty they faced every day. To me, they are the unsung heroes of society, and I salute them.

I discovered during this course that working in the community was a valuable experience to have in order to ascertain the level of care that was being delivered outside the hospital setting. It was very important to be aware of the services available for children and families. I saw that this information was important to know so that the care we delivered was holistic within the context of each patient. I came to understand that the person-centered approach is a very important part of nursing. I wanted the best care delivered to all patients regardless of age, nationality, sex, education, or economic status. I wanted to care for my patients as if they were my parents, sisters, brothers, or friends.

CHAPTER 12

Let's Do This!

You don't always need a plan.
Sometimes you just need to breathe, trust,
let go, and see what happens.

— Mandy Hale

OUR SENIOR YEAR WAS COMING to an end. We were given two weeks' vacation before our graduation day. Lai, my classmate, invited me and some other classmates to spend my vacation in her hometown, Janopol Batangas. I was left behind to help plan the graduation because I was the treasurer of the Nursing Council at the University.

I traveled to Batangas to join my friends for a weekend escapade a few weeks before graduation from nursing school. It was a hot day, so I let the wind blow and sang its song to stir my emotions — sweet memories of times gone by and hope for a good future ahead.

I have always loved the wind as it comes to me boldly and touches my skin. A cold wind rouses me to wakefulness, an alertness that makes me savor the moment. In dry weather or rain, it's the same. Soft breezes are finer than silk, smoother than water. Gales sing to the trees, sending loose leaves on a dancing, fun-fair ride. Hypnotic. Beautiful. In the summertime, the wind cools me. It allows the warmth of the sun to gently enter my muscles and bones, while my skin feels at ease with the world.

On my way to Batangas, I found myself in joyful anticipation, absorbing the bright colors of the foliage buds, taking a moment to watch a butterfly pass by, its back a brilliant electric blue. It was noon when I got to Tanauan, Batangas. I looked around to see if my friends were already at the bus station. I thought they must be running a little late. In the meantime, I enjoyed the sun, which seemed to be bringing with it free-flowing laughter, igniting a jocund glow as if a brilliant light hugged the land as the sun stretched out its golden arms. Like a child, I reached up with my hands as if they could bathe in the light. I felt sunbeams radiating all around, just like the rays of light from the heavenly bodies we adore after nightfall. Our sun. Our stars.

I was deep in the moment when I heard, "There she is, in deep contemplation." It was my friend Lai. "Tem, have you been waiting long? Sorry. We had some trouble picking up a ride from the barrio."

"Don't worry. It wasn't that long, and I entertained myself by looking at the beautiful scenery and enjoying the beautiful day," I said excitedly.

We took a jeep to Lai's place in Janopol, a barrio in Tanauan.

Janopol had great potential as a tourist site, but I appreciated it more for its glimpse into farming life. Coming from the crowded city of Manila, I could not help but admire the beauty of nature there and the simplicity of the farming lifestyle. Vegetables and fruits were available from people's backyards. The air was fresh. Birds were chirping in the treetops. The golden color of the vast rice fields signaled the coming of the harvest season. Beautiful flowers grew in people's gardens, and I could feel their hospitality in my bones.

In this place, my friends and I were very happy. This vacation was a real break from our hectic life in school, and our simple needs were well taken care of. We had plenty of food, comfortable beds, and friends to enjoy. We walked in the woods and splashed in the springs and made nilupak, a traditional, Filipino coconut dessert.

My happiness there started as a tingle in my fingers and toes, much like the feeling I have when I am anxious, but instead of being worrisome, it was warm. I felt it pass through me like a warm ocean wave washing away all my stress. The more I focused on it, the more intense it became, like a beam of light to the soul. It was infectious. We were all happy here.

Out of the blue one day, Lai asked us, "Hey, why don't we work here so we can all be together?"

"What? Are you kidding me?" asked Letty. "Who will hire us? We haven't graduated yet."

"Oh, no," Lai said. "It will be our internship while we wait for graduation."

After some discussion, Letty said, "You know what? I think that is a good idea. We can gain experience that might help us pass our board exams. What do you think, Thelma?"

I said, "Okay," but whispered silently to myself, "No one is going to hire us."

The next day, we set off for Lipa City, Batangas, to apply for nursing positions at San Sebastian Hospital. It was a quiet day, a day in which feathers without hurry moved this way and that in the air, happy to change direction according to the wind. Yet between each moment of movement was freedom, an infinitely branching path that was no path at all. In that complete liberty was a need for a calm kind of patience, the kind that is content to wait for the path to glow, to show itself worthy of adventure, curiosity, enchantment. Yes, I needed this quiet day for a new adventure because adventure never grabs you and says, "You're coming with me." It simply tells you the beginning of the story and asks if you want to follow the trail.

Yes, San Sebastian Hospital needed nurses. The nurses there were getting ready to leave for the States. "Great timing," I said to myself. The head nurse then appeared and asked us if we were ready for interviews. My classmates all answered, "Yes!"

"What?" I thought. "Are you crazy?"

I heard the head nurse say, "Okay, then."

"Oh, no," I said to myself. "There is no way out."

My first job interview was an experience I will never forget. My anxiety level increased to the point of panic during the fifteen minutes I spent in the lobby. After all, I thought, this could be the beginning of a process that would change my life forever. I became agitated, sweat moistened my forehead, and as I glanced up at the ceiling, terror took over. With so much on my mind, I could not gather my thoughts. All I could do was sigh, take a deep breath, and pray.

Despite my anxiety, the interview went well. In fact, we all were hired!

The rest of my classmates were so excited about this new employment even though it was more like an internship. We were not even looking for jobs; we were just on a short vacation and ended up employed only a couple of weeks before graduation. For my friends, the start of a new adventure like this was a time for excitement, but not for me. It was a time full of dread. I did not sleep all night, thinking, "What did we do? Are we crazy?"

Letty noticed my anxiety and said, "Don't worry. All will be well."

"How do you know?" I asked in a serious tone.

"Because I know," she answered with a grin.

Worry overcame me. I worried about having to meet new people in the area. The thought that this place was completely new to me filled me with dread. I worried that everything was different here. What would we eat? Where would we eat? And what about home? I would miss home. I worried about the hospital procedure manual and not understanding some of the technical words. I was afraid I would look like I didn't know what I was doing. My head was spinning. My brain felt like it was shutting down. I was unable to think.

Letty took my hand and held it. "I brought you some water to help ease your anxiety," she said. "Please take it before the head nurse comes." And then she said very firmly, "There is no backing out now."

Hmm. I got it. I looked at the excitement on the faces of all my friends and knew right then that with their help I could do anything. I drank the water Letty had given me and felt better.

"Thank you, Letty. I feel better now," I said, and my lips curved into a smile. "Let's do this!"

CHAPTER 13

Adventures in Lipa City

The most incredible adventure is what lies ahead.

— Anonymous

THE ADVENTURE BEFORE ME WAS a song that whispered to my soul and spoke of great new things on the horizon. It grinned at me as a new friend, as if my new friend knew the answer was yes before she asked. I welcomed my journey with a strong heart. I stood tall and loved the fresh air that came from following this melody that pulled me ever onward. I strode forward in bold steps, feeling a sense of pride in each one. This journey was not about the destination, or a finish line, for there was no such thing. This journey was about the adventure itself, about my companions along the way, and the reason for my noble struggle. My friends and I had a compass to guide us on our path, and we had strong feet to tread it. My journey couldn't promise comfort, but there was much to kindle the soul and bring the sort of joyful light I thought belonged only to the stars. I sure had a great adventure in Lipa City!

San Sebastian Hospital was founded by two members of the Dimayuga family, a brother and sister who were graduates of schools of medicine in the United States and who came home to help care for the sick in Lipa. I thought they were both beautiful people who dedicated their lives to serving the people in their hometown and that it was a very noble thing to do for our country. They treated their patients and employees as family, and it was an honor to be working there. The Dimayugas inspired us to be better learners and gave us the experience usually given only to the more privileged. For that, I am truly grateful.

Our teachers at San Sebastian inspired us with love and enthusiasm. They provided us with specialized training in the care of the sick and the care of their families and friends as well. We were taught to use our voices to speak up for our betterment and were encouraged to take part in finding answers to problems. Our voices were heard, and solutions were found.

One day, a doctor asked me, "Thelma, do you like the food being served at your dorm?"

"No, doctor," I answered.

"Why not?" he asked.

"Doctor, they always serve us tuna fish — every day, no variety."

"Oh, really?" he said. "Okay. All of you schedule a meeting with the cook to tell her what could help you enjoy the meals."

"Thank you so much, doctor. We will do that."

From then on, we enjoyed our meals every time. We were grateful.

We became all-around nurses at San Sebastian. We became experts in all of the different areas of nursing — educational, medical, surgical, adult nursing, geriatric nursing, pediatric nursing, OB-GYN nursing, and taking care of newborns. We also became experts in public health.

We learned to organize ourselves not only for the daily routine of nursing but also to be ready to perform in emergencies. For that, we needed to learn to rely on and cooperate with each other, and this trust and interdependence developed into a kind of friendship that lasted forever.

There were days when the hospital was so busy that we worked double shifts. One day, I was on my way to the dorm after working a hard day shift. The hot cement had me dancing along a little faster than usual, but my destination was near. The sun was brilliant in a cornflower-blue sky as if one perfect petal was stretched wide around the world. I reached my dorm room and was almost in a place called dreamland when I heard a loud voice calling from outside the window.

"Tem, wake up! I need help!" It was Letty.

"What is it?" I asked as I tried to wake from my slumber.

"I need help! There are several patients with stab wounds. I need nurses for the operating room and admissions."

"Okay," I said. "I will bring Susan to help in OR, and I will be there to help in admissions."

That kind of situation happened a lot, and we helped each other every time, which helped us develop the expertise we needed and gave us a head start for our future careers.

Lipa City is known as the Little Rome of the Philippines. The presence of numerous houses of worship and many religious sisters and brothers helped shape the religious consciousness and deep spirituality of the people living there, including mine. I learned that being a nurse was not easy, and I needed help from above to give me the strength I needed to do the job. There was a church in Lipa where I went to pray and ask for guidance — Our Lady of Mount Carmel. It was also a monastery.

There is a miracle story about this church, although it was controversial. In 1948, a postulant named Teresita Castillo claimed that the Blessed Mother had appeared to her several times and at times showered rose petals of "exceptional sweetness" in and around the rooms of the nuns. She said the Blessed Mother had asked for a renewal of faith throughout the country. It is said that when she appeared to Castillo for the last time, the Blessed Mother said, "I am the Mediatrix of All Grace," and many healings occurred.

This church became my sanctuary, a place of prayer for me, and it influenced me by making me want to become a nun. I decided not to entertain any suitors while I was in Lipa. My heart was focused on the heart of Jesus and helping the poor and needy.

My Lipa adventure was not just about my job. More importantly, it was about my life with my friends and the people *we* met. I knew that the journey of life was less interesting when you travel it alone. I found friends among the doctors, my coworkers, my classmates, and others I dealt with at the hospital and outside the hospital. My everyday experiences with my friends

— hanging out with each other, traveling together to explore new places, and enjoying our hobbies together — enriched my life in Lipa City. We watched each other's backs and guided each other to the pathway of happiness and joy. We became one family in a spirit of friendship and trust. As friends, we learned to share, love, and care. We became each other's support and a shoulder to lean on. My adventure in Lipa City was an unforgettable event in my life as it taught me the real meaning of life outside my home. I will be forever grateful for the experience the Lord gave me.

CHAPTER 14

It Is Time to Say Goodbye

Goodbye may seem like forever.
Farewell is the end,
but in my heart is the memory,
and there you will always be.

— *Walt Disney*

GRADUATION IS A TIME OF transition, of transformation, of significant change. The joy of graduation is sweet and mellow, a sense of growing confidence that perhaps had to struggle to bloom. To me, graduation meant I could now help change the world and change the way I approached things. I had hoped, though, that this would be easy to do. The hard part was finding the courage to walk away from the easy path. I knew that change, as always, is only for the brave of heart and for those who have a true desire to create a better world.

The night before the big day, the day when I would graduate with great pride and jubilation, I looked up in the sky as I rested in bed and awaited dreams to dance into my nighttime brain and bring an adventure of stillness and mirth. I watched the patterns of the clouds no eye had ever seen before or would ever see again. On the other side of the glass was the ever-changing art in the sky, the clouds that brought infinite images of beauty. I was so grateful. There was something in that feeling of gratitude for all those gifts I'd received just by spending a moment gazing into the blue. I felt at peace. My graduation day would be the best day of my life.

Many people in the Philippines rightfully consider graduation day a major milestone. It is, after all, a culmination of decades of hard work and sacrifice for both the parents and the students. This was the day I had studied and worked so hard for. This was the day I would receive my Bachelor of Science in Nursing degree, a degree I could be proud of. I proudly wore my gown and graduation cap, which were decorated with my family photos. We were the lucky few who were allowed to exercise our creative spirits. Underneath my gown, I wore the dress that my mother made especially for this day as this was a day of celebration for not only me but for my whole family.

I looked around and saw my mother dressed in a long, beautifully embroidered dress. My father was well-dressed with a barong tagalog made of *piña,* or pineapple, fiber. They both looked stunning. I also saw my favorite aunt, my Tiya Seryang, wearing a beautiful dress and looking so proud and happy. I went to them to give them a hug.

"Anak, I am so proud of you," said my mother as I gave her a big hug.

"I made it, Inay. Thank you for everything."

My itay, standing so proud and tall, gave me a peck on my forehead and said, "Here is my little girl. I am so proud of what you have done with your life."

"Thank you," I said. "I love you."

As I hugged Tiya Seryang, I said, "Thank you for loving me the way you do. I love you so much." I could see how proud she was of what I had accomplished.

"I made your favorite tamales," she said. "You can take some back to Lipa."

"Thank you so much, Tiya Seryang," I said. "Did you get the fabric I bought you? It was from my first salary in Lipa."

"Oh, yes. Your inay showed me when I arrived at your house. I love it. It's beautiful. Thank you for thinking of me. Did you leave some money for yourself? That fabric is beautiful and expensive."

"Don't worry, Tiya. I got it for you. I am glad you like it. I will buy you more when I get a better salary. Okay?"

I left them looking so excited and happy, but it was time to join my classmates for the graduation ceremony. Thundering applause welcomed us as we entered the auditorium. Soon we were in line to receive our diplomas. Although the room was packed, I found my family by the stage as my name was called. I was so happy to hold my diploma in my hands!

After all of the graduates had received their diplomas, the principal asked us to stand, and she gave us a blessing for the board exam that would be coming up in July. This licensure would determine if we could practice our profession. Her blessing was helpful, I guess.

Following all of the speeches, the lights dimmed and a screen rolled down from the ceiling above the stage. A projector appeared to show us pictures of our group when we had first rolled in and during our years together. We all laughed seeing our silly selves, our nervous smiles, the years of laughter, and sleepless morning looks. When it ended, I looked around and saw my classmates in tears and smiling sadly as we all knew that life would now be different. Life would change us. I bowed my head and cried. I prayed that we would stay friends no matter what.

Walking around after the ceremony and chatting with friends brought us all an early sense of nostalgia despite feeling elated for finally conquering this mountainous task. We visited our favorite spot, a little garden behind the college of nursing, and talked about the coming exam, our life plans, and the reality of life catching up to our friendship.

Soon we had to part ways and go back to our families for a small gathering with family and friends at home. It was a happy occasion for all of the family. I had a great time.

I went to bed as soon as the last visitor had gone. I needed to wake up early to go back to Lipa for work. I was to meet the rest of my friends at the bus station at 6 a.m.

In the cloudy morning, the sky exhibited growing patches of blue, the sort of hue that is soft and bright at the same time, though beneath the sheath of cloud was a gray that deepened to steel with a leading edge of brilliant white, as if it were the pages of a new book ready for any curious eyes. So, on this day, which could bring sunshine or rain, I was hoping for both.

I met my friends at the bus station, ready for the two-hour ride to Lipa City. We were still not ready to go back but had promised the director that we would be back for duty for the three-to-eleven shift that day. So, ready or not, we were on our way. Most fell asleep on the bus right away. I kept my eyes open to see the gray road as it stretched onward, hugging the land. It was a gray that had welcomed many suns, becoming silvery as it soaked in the rays. I let my eyes absorb the hues, seeing imperfections for the first time yet feeling they were created by an artistic hand, which rendered the road all the more beautiful.

I tried to close my eyes, hoping to get some sleep even for a bit — I was scheduled to work that night — but to no avail. I had much on my mind. A fusion of feelings kept me awake, different emotions attacking all at once. I already missed my PWU friends, classmates, mentors, and campus. That wonderful part of my life was over.

This is really crazy, I thought. *Why do I miss those miserable classes and the finals, the sleeplessness, and the nervousness when I was not ready for class? Those professors made my life miserable because they wanted to make sure I was prepared for life. Isn't that weird?* But then I realized that those were the unforgettable challenging parts of my life that would be a part of me forever, and I was glad for all of them. They would become an anchor to help me in this life so new to me but one that I had been prepared for. I took a breath and smiled because I knew I would be ready.

Because I was scheduled to work the night shift, I went to bed as soon as we got to the dorm. I was deep into my slumber when I heard Susan's voice. "Tem, wake up. It's time for work."

"Okay," I answered reluctantly. "Five minutes more, Susan, please." A little later, I got up and hurriedly dressed to report for duty.

On the way to the hospital, walking distance from our dorm, I looked up to see the stars light the sky like snowflakes in the night. I smiled as I felt the wind blow my hair into a tousled mane. "How do stars move?" I whispered to myself. I arrived at my station at the hospital still thinking about the beauty of the night when Letty said to me, "Tem, let's do rounds. I need to finish my charting."

"Okay," I said.

"I started making rounds to make sure all of the patients were safe and ready to sleep. "Tonight will be a quiet night," I said to myself. Apen, our orderly, usually stayed up with me when I was on duty, so I would have him get snacks for both of us from across the street. He was only sixteen but very helpful.

The night was mostly uneventful, but every time I looked up at the stairs, I noticed a woman standing there. "Apen, please tell the lady on the stairs to go to sleep. She must be a relative of one of the patients upstairs."

Apen went to the stairs, and when he came back, he said, "Thelma, there is nobody there."

"Oh, okay. Please watch for her. When you see her, please tell her to go upstairs and go to sleep."

Apen said, "Okay, Thelma. Do you want some snacks?"

"Oh, thank you, Apen. You can have some, too, if you're hungry."

"Thank you," said Apen before leaving to get the snacks.

I continued to do my charting throughout the night and my routine rounds every hour. All night, I noticed the lady looking at me from the stairs, but every time Apen went to talk to her, she was gone. I didn't know what was going on. My shift had been uneventful until the morning except for the lady on the stairs staring at me and then disappearing every time Apen would confront her. When Lai arrived at seven a.m., I gave her a report of the uneventful night and went to the dorm to sleep. "Apen, please go to sleep, too, and thank you for your help by staying all night with me."

"You are welcome. Anytime," he said, and we parted.

I was sleeping soundly when I heard Lai's voice. "Is Tem awake? Please wake her up and tell her to get dressed and go downstairs. Her uncle is here."

Susan came in to wake me and give me the message.

"Who is there?" I asked.

"He said he is your uncle. Please change and meet him downstairs," Susan said.

"Uncle, what is going on?" I asked when I got downstairs. "Why are you here?"

"I am here to pick you up. You need to come home now," he said.

"But why?" I asked fearfully.

"Your Tiya Seryang passed away last night. They could not stop the bleeding inside her stomach."

"No, I can't believe that. She was at my graduation only yesterday," I cried. "She even made sure to bring my favorite food to bring to the dorm. No, no, this cannot be happening." I became anxious. My heart was beating fast. It was too painful. "She did not look sick," I whispered to myself. "I lost my very own cheerleader. My best friend. She was always on my side. Every time I needed help, she was always there for me every step of the way. She was the very first person I thought of when I received my first salary from my internship. I loved her so much, and she loved me." I didn't know what to do. I started banging my forehead with my fist to stop my crazy thoughts as tears slid from the corners of my eyes and my vision turned blurry. I could not breathe.

"Tem," I heard my uncle say, "you need to be strong. You need to go up and get dressed so we can go home. She is in the funeral home now, waiting for you to say your final goodbye. Your name is the last word she uttered. She loved you so much. Please do not fail her. She is waiting for you. She asked to wear the fabric you bought for her. Your mother made it into a beautiful dress."

I slowly got up to gather whatever strength was left in me and told Lai to tell the head nurse that I was leaving. On my way out, I saw Apen, eager to talk to me.

"Tem, I am sorry for your loss, and please take care. I wonder about the lady that you kept seeing last night. Maybe that was your aunt trying to say goodbye to you."

"Oh, Apen, maybe. I remember I kept telling you to tell her to go to sleep, but you couldn't see her every time you tried. Oh, Lord, maybe she was trying to let me know that she was leaving me."

"Maybe."

With that thought, we left to go home.

The bus rocked us from side to side as we traveled the familiar road, our minds given to daydream or rest. There were those in the bus who chanted, their voices rising and blending in the sweet ritual of friends. Some were absorbed in music, others in worries that would erase themselves on arrival. But for me, this trip transported me back to childhood with my favorite aunt. As it passed in my mind's eye, I barely saw it all, as if I were painting a picture over a picture to show what it could be if it were restored. Call me nostalgic, but there was love in that old design.

CHAPTER 15

Caution and Congratulations!

True friends are never apart, maybe
by distance but never in heart.

— Helen Keller

IT WAS A BEAUTIFUL DAY at San Sebastian Hospital in Lipa City. It was a bright morning. I hummed a tune as I got ready for my morning shift, wondering if anybody noticed the sky and how blue it was. I wondered if they saw the serenity of the clouds that sailed by, gently moving on toward anywhere the wind wished to bring them. I wondered if they let their eyes rest upon their white edges or followed the infinite grays that blended so harmoniously. I wondered if, as I did, they imagined them to be beluga whales swimming through a clean ocean as a happy family singing and playing. If they did, I hoped they felt a little of what I felt, a calm sense of awe as warm as the rays of the sun. I hoped they felt their senses heightened, a tingle in their fingers, noticing the aroma of flowers blooming, the subtle movement of leaves, the light reflected from both foliage and feathers. When I tune in to these subtle and many pleasures, these everyday delights and wonders, nature gives me a quiet joy, and at that moment, I am happy as any queen or king has ever been.

The hospital was busy the night before with a lot of admissions. I was about to get the report from the night-duty nurse, who happened to be Letty, when Dr. Rosales came to me and said, "Thelma, please go to the meeting room first before you get the report."

"Okay, Doctor." Dr. Rosales was the resident doctor. He reminded me of a tall, jolly Santa Claus at the mall, always with a big smile and very protective of us. He became our big brother bear. *Hmm, I wonder what this meeting is for*, I thought. *Too early for a meeting.*

When I got to the meeting room, I found everyone talking about some incident the previous night. They stopped when I walked into the room. "What is this meeting all about?" I asked.

"It's about you," Dr. Rosales answered.

"About me? What did I do?" I asked, my heart pounding in terror. I looked around the room for an answer.

"Oh, Thelma, this meeting is about you being safe," Dr. Rosales said. "I called this meeting so everybody would be aware of a patient who was admitted last night. He ran into a moving vehicle on purpose just so he could be admitted here to be able to talk to you. He claimed he has been sending you a telegram every day but has received no response from you. He also tried to see you, but you did not want to see him. Please make sure you don't enter his room by yourself, okay? And for everybody here, let us make sure Thelma is safe at all times. I heard he is very rich and influential, so be careful."

Dr. Rosales then said to me, "By the way, why do you not want to see anybody? I know he is not the only one who wants to visit you."

"I want to be a nun, Doctor, so I do not want to entertain any suitors," I explained. I came out of that room with a sigh of relief because I had friends here who were willing to protect me, and I felt so lucky to have people like them by my side. Letty gave me the report of the day, but before she left, she said to me, "Tem, be careful. That guy might kidnap you. Maybe it's better for you to go back home."

"Maybe," I said to her and then thought, *Why don't these guys leave me alone?*

The time had come for us to take the board exam, a ticket for us to be employed as registered nurses and get real jobs. The Philippine Nurse

Licensure Examination was five hundred multiple-choice questions meant to test our level of competency in basic nursing and other related disciplines. We took the test for four days straight.

I did not fear the test itself because all of us had been studying every day. In the Philippines, the names of the people who pass the examination are printed in the newspapers. My fear was that I would not see my name in the newspaper when the results were released. My itay, I was sure, would wake up early that day to search for my name.

"Itay, do not buy any newspapers, please," I said to him before the test. "You have enough sons and daughters who made it, so don't even bother looking for my name."

My itay said, "Don't worry. Just relax. All will be fine."

I was so stressed out when the test days came that I had developed a big boil on my left thigh. I could hardly sit during the test. I thought I would fail.

Before I went back to Lipa to finish my internship and await the results of the board exam, I told my mother about the incident with the "suitor." She was worried and said, "Tem, you'd better come home as soon as you can. You could be in danger there."

"*Opo*, Inay," I said to pacify her. I returned to Lipa and discovered the suitor had not stopped sending me telegrams every day, but I still refused to see him or read his telegrams. "Please, Lord, let him stop. Please find him another girl to love," I prayed.

Morning arrived as gently as a mother's palm inviting the beautiful dream of the night to enter the bright day. There was more joy in the part of me that showed in the window of my eyes. There was more love and kindness awaiting a chance to skip and hop in the air from the silence of my soul. This was a beautiful sight, as the morning came as if the light had an inner beam.

I was busy making rounds when Letty phoned me from the dorm to say, "Tem, we have a visitor from PWU. One of our teachers is here. Please come to the dorm at once."

"Hmm," I said silently. "I wonder what she wants. She must be here visiting." I hurriedly went to the dorm.

"Congratulations, nurses. You all passed the board," the visitor said when she saw me in the doorway. "And a big hooray for you, Thelma. You not only passed the board, but you also topped it!"

Wow! I thought. *Thank you so much, Lord. Now I hope my itay did buy a newspaper.* (It must have been in the newspaper because the persistent suitor had sent me a congratulations telegram besides his daily one.)

That moment will linger in my mind forever because now I had in my hand the tool to achieve my goal. I was so thrilled because I realized that happiness is a rosebud that grows into a beautiful flower so intimately, one moment at a time. I was at peace.

I did decide to leave the hospital earlier than the others in order to be safe. I knew that I would miss them all — my protectors, my friends. I was so blessed to have them all in my life. I will never forget them.

Back in Manila, I was able to attend the oath-taking ceremony at the PWU School of Nursing. The ceremony unfolded with great enthusiasm. An oath-taking ceremony involves making a solemn promise before an institutional authority. It is more than a promise to yourself and another person. The person under oath is expected to comply with any oath they take regarding their future behavior. It marked a significant beginning, a new life, a new step to a better future, a readiness to take on the responsibilities given only to a few.

I received congratulations for work well done from school officials and my former classmates and teachers. Our dean hugged me and asked, "What are your plans, Thelma?"

"I do not have any plans yet, ma'am," I said. "I just got back home. I want to spend quality time with my parents for a little while."

"Okay, then. Let me know when you are ready. I have a teaching position ready for you."

Soon after our conversation, she sent one of the faculty to convince me to teach in one of the schools of nursing in Manila. At this time in my life, I weighed only seventy-five pounds, stood only four foot, eleven, and wore no makeup. I looked like a student, not a teacher.

"Thelma, I came to convince you to teach in one of the schools of nursing in Manila. You are highly recommended by the dean and faculty of the university as well as the officials at San Sebastian Hospital in Lipa City. Topping the board exam is a wonderful addition to your résumé. But you look so young, you could easily be mistaken as a freshman student. That is not much of a problem though. All you have to do is dress like one of the faculty members. You need to dress a little older than your age. Wear heels, wear eyeglasses, put on a little makeup to look like a faculty member. Okay?"

Oh, my, I thought. *I can't even walk in high heels. And eyeglasses? I don't use them. Makeup? Oh, no. I don't think this will work.*

I told her I would think about it and let her know.

My sister Luz had been dreaming of my coming to be with her in Guam. She had been telling my mother about a job opportunity at the hospital there and that I would be earning more in Guam because I would be paid in dollars. I knew she was trying to help me get a job there. With that in mind, I told my dean that I wouldn't be able to teach because I was planning to leave the country soon.

I applied to be a private duty nurse so I would have the freedom to resign anytime; I wouldn't have a contract requiring that I stay, so I could leave if I chose to go to Guam. The only problem was that our phone at home was not connected yet. I needed a phone so the hospital could notify me if a family needed a private nurse for their ill relatives. So my father asked Roland, our neighbor and an admirer since I was twelve years old, for help because his family was the only one on the block who had a telephone. He agreed and walked to our house every time the hospital called for a nurse, hoping to talk to me. His effort, however, was to no avail. I never talked to him. Now I wish I had. He could have been a good friend. He always reminded me of setting off firecrackers in front of my family's house every Christmas. He waited for my friendship for almost thirteen years, and I wish him well. I wish life had a rewind button because then maybe he could be my friend. I do hope he found somebody to love and love him back.

CHAPTER 16

Next Stop, Guam!

If we were meant to stay in one place,
we would have roots instead of feet.

— Rachel Wolchin

IT WAS A GREAT MORNING to see what this life would bring. There was more triumph in the part of me that peeked through the skylight of my eyes. It seemed as if there were more love awaiting a chance to jump into the air in that silent sputter I sensed in my essence. This morning, there was a deep sweetness that vibrated within me, and I discovered a way to reveal that energy. Colorful, pastel sun rays shone through my bedroom window and curtains, revealing the beauty of the many colors that entwined in the curtains that I loved so much. The browns were as varied as sandbanks at dawn, as lovely as the prettiest of timber carried ashore upon windblown ripples. Surrounded by light, I saw the radiance of the morning as they signaled the start of a beautiful day, yet in truth they were powerful and well-built, giving shape and configuration. As the moments passed, their potency increased and softened, fearless and gentle, telling of the day that passed into the beyond.

Great news from my sister Ate Luz! There were two openings for registered nurses in Guam. That was surely great news for Lai and me. We could go together at the recruiter's expense. My sister said that she would submit all the necessary papers and would let us know the results as soon as she could.

In the meantime, I continued to engage in private duty nursing in a hospital setting to gain more experience and training. Private duty nurses work one on one with patients who need ongoing medical treatment due to chronic illness or injuries. I took a proactive approach, focusing on the prevention of complications. I found that the one-on-one attention offered me the peace of mind that my patient was receiving the right care at the right time.

As a private duty nurse, I learned so much about caring for the sick and the socioeconomic conditions prevalent in the country. It was my responsibility as a private duty nurse to assess and evaluate patients and provide the services they needed for their care. I collaborated with the Director of Nursing and updated each patient's plan of care and implemented it. I kept patients healthy and improved their quality of life. Wealthy patients in the Philippines hire private duty nurses. Only the rich can afford them.

When I finally got word from Guam, I learned that both Lai and I would be hired as contract workers at the hospital there. According to our contracts, we would be given free housing near the hospital for two years, we would be assigned to the ward or clinic according to our expertise and capabilities, and we would receive our salary every two weeks and be paid in U.S. dollars.

Lai and I were so excited about having our own place to stay. "Inay," I said, "we will have a place to stay and be independent. I am so looking forward to this arrangement. I really want us to be on our own so we can learn everything. I am so excited to do this."

"Okay," my inay said calmly.

But something was bothering me. "I really do not want to be with my sister at this point in my life," I told my mother. "I do not know her. I don't remember ever being with her in the Philippines. I was always with my brothers. I don't even know how to act or talk to her. The only memory I have of her is when occasionally she would come home from her dorm. She always wanted to either cut or comb my hair. We never had any bonding at all. I do not know her at all."

I couldn't sleep thinking about staying with Ate Luz and prayed that my mother would understand my dilemma. While waiting for the results of the recruitment process, I spent sleepless nights thinking about my future in Guam. I promised myself that I wouldn't stay with my sister if I could help it. To me, she was a stranger. I knew my brothers better. I started to have anxiety attacks just thinking I would be with her. Sad but true.

I started having scary thoughts and bad dreams. There were times I awoke with tears in my eyes, I was so afraid to face my sister. What would I say to her? I felt trapped. Everything and everyone showed me that all would be fine, but I was still anxious. The fear would come out of nowhere, like an electrical storm in my consciousness. And it was quite painful, not like a toothache but as some terrible sorrow. Maybe it was a sort of deep, frozen anxiety with nowhere to go as my heart kept saying, "Help me!" My soul was in a state of unbearable pain and misery.

I knew I could not go on like that. I decided to have a heart-to-heart talk with my mother.

"Inay, I really do not know what to do," I said with tears in my eyes. "I really do not want to stay with my sister."

"Anak," my mother answered, again in a calm voice, "you and your sister are in the same boat. She wants you and Lai to stay with her for two reasons. One is to get to know you, and the second is to make sure you are safe. Why don't you give yourself a chance to know her? If you don't get along, you will still have a chance to find another place to stay when you are in Guam."

"That makes sense," I said. "Okay, then. I will stay with her, and if I cannot feel comfortable, I will move."

"I guess that is a fair deal," my mother said. "I will tell her about our conversation, and we will start from there. Okay?" Then she hugged me.

I felt better after that talk. It gave me the confidence to conquer my fear. I hoped and prayed that this was a start to transforming my anxiety, turning it into personal power and peace of mind. I decided to stay with my sister and finally give this relationship a chance.

The day we left for Guam, we got up early to go to the airport in Manila. I was so excited. This would be my very first time on a plane. In the car, I looked at my itay's face. He looked tired, and he looked older than usual. He was still handsome, a Spanish descendant, a mestizo. He also looked sad. I said, "Itay, are you okay? You look tired."

"Anak, I am just thinking about all my children. After school, everybody leaves to find adventure in other places. All I do is take you all to the airport. I will not have a girl at home when you leave. I will surely miss you, Anak."

"Don't worry, Itay. One day, I will take you to America. Yes, one day. I promise," I said to pacify his sadness.

My mother, too, was looking away from me to not show her tears. "Oh, Inay, don't worry about me. I will do my best so you can be proud of your baby girl," I said.

"I will pray for you always," my inay said. "And remember, we love you so much. We believe in your capabilities to do great things. Please be as sweet as you are and always believe in the Lord above to help you. Be strong, and be brave. Our prayers will be with you always."

"Thank you, Inay. I will do that. I love you so much too. I promise one day I will take you both to where I am so we can be together again." I saw my parents' faces light up, and I calmed down and said a prayer of thanksgiving.

There were many people at the airport. I looked around and saw Lai's family and some classmates who were there to send us off. Letty, Zeny, and Letty's mom were there. Ine, my niece, was there, too, wearing a PWU uniform. She also wanted to be a nurse. Lai and I were wearing striking dresses made of jusi, a traditional, sheer fabric hand-loomed from abaca fibers and displaying beautiful embroidery sewn by my mother's dressmakers. Our friends gave us some orchid leis that smelled so sweet. It was a wonderful small gathering of hearts and well-wishers. Nanay Choleng, my brother-in-law Angel's mother, came to us and said calmly, "The employees of Pan Am are going on strike now, but I will try my best to get you on the plane today." Then she left.

Uh-oh, I thought. *Maybe we're going to Guam some other day.* But I remained calm. I watched other passengers being told about the strike. People were angry and frustrated because many of them had to leave that day, not any other day. I could feel the frustrations that were building up all around the airport, slowly affecting us. My mother asked, "What is happening?" I told her the Pan Am employees were going to strike, so no plane was going anywhere that day.

"Oh, it's okay," my inay said happily. "This way, we will have you with us for a while until after the strike. I like that."

But Nanay Choleng, a very influential person with the airline, returned and whispered to me, "Come, Thelma and Lai. Say goodbye to your families quietly, and then come with me."

We said goodbye as fast as we could and followed Nanay Choleng to the luggage area, and the airport personnel took us to the plane. We were pointed not to the passenger section but the cockpit.

"Wow!" I said in excitement. "We are with the pilots!"

We took our seats and buckled our seatbelts as the plane prepared to take off. As it accelerated, my heartbeat was in sync with the pulsing sound of the engines. The jet gathered speed and took off, almost immediately providing a spectacular sight of my beloved home. We left our hearts in the city of our ancestors. The pilots were so nice to us and instructed the stewardess to give us the same special food that they were served. They even offered us wine with lunch, which we refused. All in all, it was a great experience for someone on her very first flight across the ocean.

CHAPTER 17

Extraordinary Friendships Fill My Days

May everlasting peace reign o'er us.
May Heaven's blessing to us come.
Against all peril, do not forsake us.
God protect our isle of Guam.

— *Stand Ye Guamanians*, regional anthem of Guam

WHEN WE ARRIVED IN GUAM, we were immediately treated to scenes of nature, though it was hot from the bright sun rays. The sun was direct, with a temperature in the eighties, but it felt hotter because of the higher humidity. The day opened as if its gleam itself was an entrance into a dreamworld, my hope, my shining star that formed a strand and opened me to the possibilities of a better future.

My sister Ate Luz, her husband, Angel, and their boys — George (five years old), Glenn (four years old), and our little Angel (three years old) — were there to pick us up. They were very surprised that we made it in spite of the strike.

"I did not expect you to come today," Ate Luz said. "The telegram from Pan Am said that the strike is on today."

"Lola Choleng had many connections at the airport," I said gratefully. "She was able to put us both in the cockpit of the plane before the strike started. No runway for us. We made it onto the plane through the cargo loading area."

"We'll let you rest today," Ate Luz said, "and we will see the sister on Monday. She will really be surprised." She was referring to Sister Claire, the headmistress of the hospital where we would be working. "She will also say, 'What are these two young girls doing here? So young and skinny, like little girls.'"

We just giggled.

"Okay, let's go home," Ate Luz directed us.

Their house was fifteen minutes from the airport. No traffic there. It was a beautiful ride to Tumon Heights, a very nice community in Guam. My sister bought her house from our sister Ate Remy when Ate Remy left for the United States. It was a four-bedroom ranch house, nicely furnished, with a big gathering room. Ate Luz showed us the room Lai and I would share. It was beautiful and spacious.

"This is for you both. Make it your own," my sister said. "You can rest now, and we will have a get-together tonight so you can meet some friends."

With that, I knew that I would like it there. My sister and brother-in-law were both very warm and friendly.

Lai and I took our much-needed rest and then met many very interesting people. Among them were Dante and Lily Navarro and their daughter, Arlene. Dante and Lily had met each other in Saigon before the Vietnam War. Dante was an engineer working at the Black Construction Company with my brother-in-law, Angel. Dante was a handsome man, full of energy, who liked to sing and had a great voice. Truly a family man, he also helped his parents in the Philippines. Lily was a beautiful woman, very fair complexioned, with gracious gestures and a lovely smile. She was a very good cook and an accountant by profession.

I also met Emmon, an engineer and the brother of my Kuya Angel. He was very good-looking, a little shy, and liked to drink beer. He was also a cheerful fellow; when he smiled, his face beamed.

My Kuya Angel was a very quiet and caring person with a wonderful sense of humor. He was also very smart and was vice-president of the company. My sister Luz was a beautiful woman, very intelligent, a leader, and the head of public health in Guam. She was tall, about five feet, two inches, and carried herself well.

My friend Lai was my best friend for life. She, too, was beautiful, though a little skinny, with tantalizing eyes like Natalie Wood's. She was very reserved, but her eyes sparkled at the sight of her latest crush.

We had a great time meeting these new people and hoped we would meet more as the days went on.

That weekend, I decided to learn more about Guam and Guam Memorial Hospital. I learned that Guam is a very small island, 210 square miles, but the largest of the Mariana Islands and a territory of the United States. It is a beautiful island with white-sand beaches and is a popular vacation spot. It is also rich in history and culture. The indigenous people are called Chamorrans, and their unique culture is still alive.

What interested me most, though, was that the major health issue in Guam was the presence of amyotrophic lateral sclerosis (ALS), a disease also known as Lou Gehrig's Disease, named after a famous New York Yankees ballplayer who lost his life to it. The incident rate of this disease was very high, high enough to have one strain of the disease named the Guamanian strain. A study conducted from 1947 to 1952 showed that all of the patients admitted to the hospital for ALS in that time period were Chamorrans. Further studies show that the ingestion of food derived from the false sago palm (Cycas micronnesica) contributed to the development of ALS.

What I learned about Guam Memorial Hospital was that it was built at Oka Point in 1956. That marked a major change in the local government's role in the delivery of medical care to the community. For many years, the United States government had provided free hospital and health care services to the people of Guam. The U.S. Navy took on that responsibility in 1898, when the United States took formal possession of Guam. It continued those services until after World War II, when it donated the first Guam Memorial Hospital facility to Guam's Department of Public Health and Welfare.

In 1964, the hospital was established as a line agency of Guam's executive branch. The 230-bed hospital offered acute, psychiatric, and long-term services. The hospital was a memorial hospital because it was built to honor the memory of the Chamorrans who suffered for their support of the United States during the war. There was a nursing shortage at the hospital when Lai and I applied, so our timing was perfect.

I was so glad I had some time to familiarize myself with my place of work and gain some understanding of this island. That helped me adjust to my new job as well as to the culture of the island. It made me feel better about meeting hospital officials.

The day I met Sister Claire, the headmistress of the hospital, was a good day. I felt the enchantment of birth in the early morning, a sense of an old soul reawakening to fashion together all that was worthy. It was hot but gorgeous. A little windy but cloudless, signaling a great day ahead. I went to the office to see Sister Claire. She was beautiful but modest and fervent, very peaceful and gentle. She commanded respect.

She stood up to greet me and said, "Hello, Miss Garcia. I see you made it in spite of the strike. I am so proud of you. Welcome to Guam Memorial Hospital." She grabbed my hand for a warm handshake. This was the start of my two-year job on this beautiful island and the beginning of the development of my career.

Guam was a very small dot in the world, but this little island gave me a life of magic. I awakened every morning to a new life that came as a sea breeze, flipping over and air-kissing me with a coldness that brought joy and happiness with an awareness of every moment. This tiny dot gave me a lot of experiences. This was the place where I created a new life rooted in love and nurtured by good friends, where I found the cool winds and rain refreshing. A place to experience all of my firsts — my first freedom of expression, my first salary (to share with my family), my first dance for charity, my first outdoor movie, my first bowling win, my first watch, my first patient with ALS (who made me realize that life was too short to waste), my first Valentine's Day dance, my first-ever tears shed for love, and many more firsts that made my life full. I grew stronger in every storm and welcomed the sunny days as a time to make solid progress. My life there was an inspiration. In that little paradise, I learned that life is not the last sentence on the last page; it is the sweet text that appears on all the pages, one letter at a time. That brought me great peace of mind every moment of each day.

Guam could be boring to some, but for me, it was a great place to enjoy family and friends. I made it a paradise, a wonderland. It was my refuge, as modest as any hill or as grand as any great design. It became an aurora, a sunrise, a concert, a colorful sunset that brought a feeling of inner peace and harmony to my soul. This wonderful place became more appealing once I met more friends, including Fred, Pat, Sherry, Lolit, and Untog. They made life beautiful. Together, we wrote a great story on the innermost pages of our souls. It was the poetry that bonded us together. We cared for each other and took care of each other's needs with care and understanding as we developed not as friends but as a family.

As a family, we built a place in our souls of golden rocks, a sort of court-yard, with the sun to keep it warm and to keep the foliage evergreen. There, our love was a fountain of cool water, and the birds thrived with happy songs. We had given each other the key, so we became a family with an eternal membership certificate. And so I present Angel and Luz Abcede, Dante and Lily Navarro, Mr. and Mrs. Baby Borja, Ninong Malixi, Uncle Pace, Fred, Pat, Lolit Sherry, Lai, and last but not least, Untog. I loved all of their beautiful personalities. I wanted to paint a picture in my mind of them so I wouldn't forget any of them.

Where do I begin? So many stories and events to share. Shall I begin with the story about our trip to Cocos Island with my Ate Remy and Kuya Jun and their kids — Blossom, Ace, and Amour? Or with the story about the beauti-ful boat built by all the master engineers of the Black Construction Company in Guam? That boat had been in the making for months and stayed in the backyard of our house to witness our merriment and dancing, our picnick-ing on Christmas Day, and the many more parties we held in that place. The boat stayed, waiting to be launched one day, to witness our fun and laughter.

If only that boat could talk! It would tell of all the different personalities in our makeshift family. It would speak of Fred, a man of medium height with brown eyes and a great laugh, who possessed the power to brighten the day. Our protector and brother in crime, he was an engineer working for Xerox at the airbase.

It would share stories about Pat, a beautiful lady with a great chuckle of joy. She was a nurse who played the piano with gusto.

Or it would tell of Untog, a great guy who had come to Guam with a dream of helping his family. He was orphaned at three and lost his best friend, his brother, when he was in high school. He stood five-foot-four, and some people considered him handsome. He was reserved but became our friend. He truly loved his work in Guam. Together with the rest of my friends and engineers, including Emmon, Dante, and others, they finally finished *the* boat — the pride and joy of the engineers, the tiny-bubbles gang, the best-in-the-West minds of the century. Finally, it was time to launch, time to test the ingenuity of the engineers, their months of hard work, and their mind-blowing design. The day had come to test the tide. The day replays itself in my mind . . .

Even the weather seemed excited to witness the grandeur. The boat was like a new blossom on a radiant spring morning. Once tightly confined on land, it could now be as free as a waving banderole in the ocean.

Coco Island, here we come! With picnic baskets, swimsuits, and the famous boat, we marched onward. Big break coming up. Take five. Relax. Sip the pink bubbles. All lights are green, and we are ready to begin! Yes, we are. "Ready, go!" Dante commanded. "Ready, go!"

"Oh no!" the spectators said. "What happened?" We watched the boat tumble over and over. It was quiet. Nobody was talking as we watched the boat sink beneath the calm surface of the water like a mini-Titanic. The precious boat was gone.

Yes, we made memories that would last a lifetime in that graceful place where beautiful friendships were made with laughter and love.

That was Guam.

CHAPTER 18

Goodbye Guam, Hello America

Be fearless; have the courage to take risks.
Go where there are no guarantees.
Get out of your comfort zone even
if it means being uncomfortable.

— *Katie Couric*

FOR TWO WONDERFUL YEARS, GUAM was a familiar and happy place for me. A home where I felt safe. A home where I felt loved and appreciated. A home where my heart was comfortable being vulnerable and real. In that place, I was calm. I loved myself and sensed a balance within myself. I was happy and content there. In the summertime, my laughter felt as colorful as English daisies in the grass. Even when I felt as if my heart and blood were frozen, it would make me warm. Guam became my shelter, my guardian, always with an open door. The keys were always in my pocket, a love that was always mine. I could have stayed there forever as I felt I belonged there in a way that was secure and deep. I accepted the land beneath my soles, and it accepted me. In that place, I felt so blessed.

It was a lovely day. The early-morning sunlight, soft and spread out, gave way to the first strong beams of the day, the rays that brought true warmth. In that gleaming light, the water evaporated in slow waves, waves that swirled in a gentle wind, flowing upward to clear white clouds. The birds were singing. Birdsong is the music of daytime as if they are murmuring their fondest memories. I was on cloud nine when I heard my name.

"Thelma, Sister Claire wants you in her office," said Gloria, my head nurse. Gloria was a beautiful lady with a generous smile. She was the embodiment of beauty and brains. She stood tall at five foot, three, with fair skin and an oval face that was dressed with an ever-cheerful smile. She was a dutiful and energetic head nurse, a true leader at heart. We got along well.

"Do you know why?" I asked, curious about the request.

"No," she said with a smile. "Uh-oh. You could be in trouble," she joked.

"Okay. Wish me luck."

Sister Claire's office was in a small building across from the main hospital. It wasn't fancy — simply a building of solid construction, a little bit like the people it served. The inside of the office was modestly furnished with a brown desk and a brown filing cabinet for employees' records and other important papers. It was clean and decorated mostly with plants. It was a very calming space.

I found Sister Claire sitting in a chair behind her neat, brown desk, looking excited to see me. Sister Claire was the director of nurses and was also responsible for nurse recruitment for the hospital. The nun was a picture of peace. She always wore a smile but was very strict when it came to our work and absenteeism.

"Thelma, congratulations! I am recommending that you renew your contract with us for another two years. Mr. Fleenor, our hospital administrator, and I are well aware of your good standing at this hospital and the great job you are doing. We are so happy with the quality of your work. We wrote to PWU to tell them what a great contribution you are making to our hospital, and we are very blessed to have you and Lai Rojas. We are so proud of you both," she said excitedly. "Please let me know what you plan to do. Congratulations again for a job well done."

"Thank you, Sister, for your time," I simply said as I left her office.

I went home happy, thinking about what to do. It was the first day of summer. I felt like I was an open book, but instead of words, the pages rendered a soft and warming light. My usual stride lengthened as if somehow I was solar-powered and my joy battery was recharged. I smiled a brilliant smile.

When I got home, I found my sister sitting at our dining table with my *ninong*, Malixi, a man we had met in Guam who had become like a second father to us. He was an engineer who had helped us in our adjustment when we were very new there. He was a wonderful man who really cared for us, and we were blessed to have him in our life.

"Hi, *Ninong*," I said.

"Hi, Thelma. How is your job?" he asked.

"Oh, *Ninong*, it is great! Sister Claire is very happy. She recommends we renew our contract here," I said joyfully.

My sister Luz heard our conversation and firmly said, "You are not thinking of staying here, right? You know you have everything you need to go to America. You have a license to work there, and your status has already changed to immigrant status."

I did not say anything as I didn't know what to do.

"What will happen to your boyfriend?" *Ninong* suddenly said.

"Boyfriend? I don't have a boyfriend, *Ninong*," I said.

My sister's reaction told me she did not want me to stay in Guam any longer. She knew I had a dream, a journey to take, and she would not stand in the way of my dreams because dreamland ideas were born of love and transformed from pure imagination into real magic, a gift of the divine.

At that moment, I knew I would be leaving. This moment had been coming for a long time, like the headlamps of some faraway train. As the train pulls into the station, there is a sense of shock. I knew in my heart that leaving would not be easy. This place had been my cocoon for two years, which for me was a lifetime. I needed a sanctuary, and I was grateful. My eyes wandered to the wooden surface of the dining table, its rosy color bright yet earthy. My hand felt the warmth of the sun. Leaving Guam, my home, was not going to be easy, yet I would take with me memories of comfort and joy.

I met with Sister Claire the next week to tell her of my decision to go to America to follow my dream and to find my way to improve my career. She was not happy, but she supported my decision and wished me luck in all of my endeavors.

"I will miss you, my dear," she said as she gave me a hug.

All I could say as I held back my tears was, "Thank you, Sister, for all your support and love. I will never forget what I have learned in this hospital."

Fred, Lai, and I decided we would all go to the United States together so we could support each other. The rest of our friends, including Pat, Lolit, and Untog, had to finish their contracts. I was truly blessed to have had such wonderful friends who always stood by me during my time in Guam. It's true what they say: "Real family does not always come from your blood. It is the people standing beside you when no one else is."

To emigrate is a one-way ticket in so many ways. When you leave a place, the world you leave carries on and evolves. The space I occupied in the lives of others was naturally filled. While I was with them, though, I changed. They changed. So, before I went on another escapade, I wanted to tell my friends and family how they helped me in my life's journey in Guam.

Dear Ate Luz and Kuya Angel,

Words are not enough to express my sincerest gratitude for having you in my life. Thank you. There are so many things I admire about the two of you. Please let me start by saying thank you for just being you. You both are confident, determined, loving, kind, and generous. Neither of you has a mean bone in your body, and neither of you has ever done anything to compromise your kind heart and tender soul. You both have been my role models, and you bravely paved the way for me to make sure I would not make the same mistakes again. I am so blessed to have you both, and I do hope you never change.

Thank you for knowing me better than I knew myself. Thank you for knowing exactly what I needed without my saying it. Thank you for being my best supporters, for believing in me, and for helping me see my potential when I failed to. Thank you both for pushing me to be a better person, a better leader. I always strive to do what I feel you would do in every situation, and if I get the sense that you would not approve, I'll probably not do it. You're my moral compass and are among those people whose union is of utmost importance to me.

I really appreciate each of you as a person, as a friend, as a sister, brother-in-law, and any other role you have in my life. Thank you both for everything. I love you both so much for making me believe I can do anything. Thank you both for always reminding me what George Bernard Shaw said: "Life isn't about finding yourself. Life is about creating yourself."

Dear Lily and Dante,

Friends like you come along once in a lifetime. I don't think I have enough words to express how much I value your friendship. I appreciate all the times you both listened to me and were there for me every time I needed someone. I remember when I was very new. Dan, the vice-president of the company, was the one who took me to the hospital for work and picked me up. I was so embarrassed to ride in the car because of your high position in the company. Dan noticed my embarrassment and said, "Thelma, don't worry. Someday you will do the same thing for someone else. You will help them the same way I am helping you. Just relax." I realized then that one day I would help somebody like me.

Thank you for all the great things you both did for me. I promise that the good things you did for me I will also do for others. Thank you for teaching me a lesson I could use on my journey. I've heard people say that friends are like precious gold, and I totally agree. You have been the gold nuggets that remind me of how valuable good friends can be. Thank you so much for being by my side no matter what. May the Lord bless and keep you always and bring you peace.

Dear Lai,

Our friendship has stood the test of time. We have shared tears, laughter, and a special kind of love, different from that of acquaintances and fair-weather friends who have passed by throughout the years. You are the person

I call when I am most in need. Oftentimes when I doubt myself, the days when I feel I could crumble to the floor, I know you are always there to pick me up from that cold floor so I can stand again. Even when I'm at my worst, you see me at my best. You are there for me when the going gets tough and when the road is rocky and dark.

To me, you are extraordinary in ways you cannot comprehend. You are the one who continues to build me up when the rest of the world tries to tear me down. You know it takes years, a lot of stress, and endless cookie dough to get to this point in our friendship, the point where not even the greatest of catastrophes can break our bond. You know my heart inside out, a skill learned through time, not overnight. I know you have sisters of your own, the ones who are the true definition of unconditional love, the ones you won't be apart from, the ones who will never be too far away. But you should know that in my heart you will always have a seat atop a pedestal. I will always be there for you because friendship like ours comes around once in a lifetime. You have filled my life with so much joy, and I pray for all your dreams to come true. I am so grateful for you in my life, and I will forever call you my best friend and the sister of my heart.

Dear Fred,

They say that friends are the family you choose. I owe you so many thank-yous, but the first is for you choosing me to be a part of your family. I knew when we first met I was just a friend of your cousin, but as days went by, you became my brother, a brother who always has my back. Thank you for always being there for me. Thank you for listening to all of my complaints as well as my dreams. Thank you for staying positive. When I am ready to give up on people or myself, you are the one telling me that things will turn around. Even when I don't want to believe it, you are sure, like I don't have a choice. And when you are right, there isn't even a hint of "I told you so." I admire the way you keep looking up even when life tries to knock you down.

Thank you for always listening. It doesn't matter if it's a drama that will be over in a week or about people you never met, you listen and you always seem to know what to say. Sometimes just being able to get stuff off my chest is the only solution I really need, and you understand that. Thank you for having my back. It's good to know I will always have someone who is there for me and won't let people mistreat me. Thank you for being you. You are a lot of things — some good, some bad — but I wouldn't change one of them. You are a perfect brother as you are. As a brother, you know me as I am. You understand where I have been, accept me for what I have become, and still allow me to grow, and I am so grateful. May all your dreams be a reality, and may the Good Lord keep you safe always.

Dear Pat and Lolit,

Your friendship means so much to me. Meeting you both made my life in Guam a very good life. The laughter, the parties, and the beautiful escapade on Cocos Island are experiences I will never forget. But it is time to move on; so, with a sad heart, I wish to say goodbye to both of you. My memories of our wonderful days of friendship I will keep in my heart to forever stay locked inside. Those great memories will serve as my guide on my newly chosen path. "Truly great friends are hard to find, difficult to leave, and impossible to forget."

Dear Sherry,

As I leave for the United States, I would like to bid you adieu and not a goodbye, for I do hope we will meet again soon. You are a wonderful person who showed me that life is beautiful.

Your laugh and wonderful stories of life always made me forget the bad times. I will remember our wonderful stories of friendship that made us one of a kind. Remember our fishing trip? Kuya Angel said, "Sherry, why are you all dressed up with all that makeup? We are going on a fishing trip, not a party." We laughed and laughed. What a great time! I bid you adieu with a heavy heart and hope to see you again some sunny day. Thank you for everything. Hope you live your dreams and attain success in all your endeavors.

Dear Untog,

This is not goodbye, my friend. This is a thank you. Thank you for coming into my life and giving me joy. I will miss you because no one will tolerate my annoying antics as you do. No one will calm me down when I am excited, listen to my daily rants, harass me with banter, or make sure I don't miss the party as you do. Remember this conversation? "Hey, you two, wake up! It's time to go to work." You were banging on our door. "We won't be able to go to the party again if you are late for work. That is the rule!" And you scratched your head in frustration. Our friendship is the best thing that ever happened to me. Talking to you made me smile, and meeting you set me free. Promise me you won't forget our laughs, our jokes, our smiles, our conversations, our fishing escapades, our wonderful experiences together, our friendship. Let us remember the beautiful memories we made together as friends. Remember what they say: "True friends never say goodbye. They just take extended leaves of absence from each other."

Let us then not say goodbye, only farewell. I wish you luck, and may all your dreams come true.

To all of the special people I met in Guam, I said this and will say it again: Thank you again, my friends, for all the love you shared with me in this beautiful place. I will remember you all. I know that for every mountain peak, there is another, yet climbing is everything. With each stretch, I reach higher. With each stride, I am stronger. I keep gaining more strength to carry me through times of hardship. I will feel the winter wind, and the cold will teach me to stay warm inside my soul. I will feel sharp rocks, and the cold will whisper to me to keep on walking. Maybe at those times, the cloud will shower me with its icy love, reminding me of the tears I prevented by walking through these difficult ways, and it will make me want to move faster. This journey does not promise me comfort, but the memories of great times and friendship will kindle my soul and bring me smiles.

Until this time of transition, I felt like I had been a backseat passenger in my own life. Now I am holding the wheel and have my own set of keys. I had thought it would be exhilarating to finally have them in my hands. Yet years after I won my independence, I pretended that someone, anyone but me, was doing the driving. I am tough.

And now I feel it's time to turn the radio on to let some tunes that feel joyful and free seep into my soul. Maybe someday someone else will come alongside me, someone else who has his own keys and plays his own song. Maybe he will stay a while and make this open road a friendlier place. Maybe someday. But for now, I will drive my own car, two hands on the wheel, setting my own navigation system, choosing my own tunes. And now I bid you adieu.

CHAPTER 19

The Healing Power of Love

Your support network is the solid ground
from which you can propel yourself upwards.

— *Anna Barnes*

EVEN THOUGH THE DAWN WAS still some time away, there was a light in my heart that had been missing just the day before. There was a spark of hope, a ray of sunshine yet to be born, but it was there and I could feel it. Perhaps that was optimism, the anticipation of the goodness to come. It was a feeling I had not had since I'd left Guam, and it felt as foreign as it felt welcomed. Yes, we had arrived in America, landing in San Francisco.

San Francisco was very different from Guam. It began in 1776 as a Spanish mission and presidio, then became a part of Mexico, and then was ceded to the United States at the end of the Mexican-American War in 1848. The California Gold Rush of 1849 brought people to the city until 1906, when an earthquake and fire killed thousands, left more than two hundred thousand homeless, and destroyed three-quarters of the city. The city was quickly rebuilt, though, to become prosperous, powerful, and popular. Think of San Francisco and you think of the Summer of Love, beatniks, hippies, an active civil rights movement, anti-war demonstrations, the rise of black power and gay rights, cable cars, the Golden Gate Bridge, Chinatown, and Alcatraz. It is also a beautiful city with lots of culture — museums, theater, opera, symphony — and world-class cuisine.

We arrived in San Francisco in the late 1960s, the decade some claim was the best decade in the area's history. San Francisco was the place to come to for those looking to "tune in, turn on, drop out." Yes, this place was very different from where I came from. Guam was nothing compared to this beautiful city. Funny, though, how my thoughts were still with that place I had called home.

Those who arrived from Guam with me were my sister Luz and her three boys, Lai, and Fred. My sister Remy's husband picked us up at the airport and took us to their home in Sunnyvale, forty miles from San Francisco.

"Oh my, the boys are getting so big now," Remy said of our nephews when she saw us. "Thelma, Lai, Fred, welcome to the U.S. Thelma, I do hope you can find a job here in Sunnyvale so we can get to know each other better. I haven't seen you since you were twelve years old."

"That *is* the plan," I answered.

We all decided to enjoy ourselves and see some of California before we settled in to work.

Remy and my brother-in-law Pappy had a camper, a recreational motor vehicle that included living quarters and a kitchen. I had never seen a camper, so I was excited to try it out. We traveled to different places in California, such as Lake Tahoe, Yosemite National Park, and the redwood forests near Eureka. It was a wonderful experience, one I will never forget. California has so much to offer, including a coastline of beautiful beaches. I was grateful I had not stayed in Guam.

After we explored California, Fred, Lai and I decided to visit New York, where we met up with a classmate and good friend of ours to explore the "Big Apple." Described often as the economic and cultural capital of the world — it is the most populous city in the United States — New York is also known as the "City That Never Sleeps." We enjoyed New York but found it too big for us, so we came back to sunny California after only a one-week visit.

Lai and I started to look for jobs in San Francisco, a city a little bit calmer than the Big Apple. It was only an hour or so from Sunnyvale, so it was easy to visit Ate Remy on the weekends. I wanted to get to know my sister and her family and to reconnect after all the years we were so far apart — in age as well as distance. I never saw her in my growing-up years; she was about twenty years older than I. She was truly beautiful — petite and slender with a welcoming smile and beautiful eyes that spoke to my soul. I wanted to know her better and to show her that I loved her every day.

My brother-in-law was a handsome guy, taller than most Filipinos, very friendly and welcoming. I knew right away that he was a good man. I knew that they would both support me in all my undertakings in life. Knowing that brought me peace.

The job-hunting day arrived, igniting our rainbow world. On this bright day, I had a sense of serenity, a peace that had invited itself into my soul and made itself at home. I was very confident that Lai and I would find good jobs in the heart of San Francisco. We saw that the Veterans Hospital on Clement Street in the Richmond District was looking for nurses, so we went to check out what might be in store for us there. The San Francisco Veterans Affairs Medical Center had the largest-funded research program in the Veterans Health Administration and was a teaching hospital for the University of California, San Francisco's School of Medicine. It was so much bigger than Guam Memorial Hospital.

When we arrived, we were scheduled for an interview right away. "Hmm, they badly need help," I said. "I was hoping to find a place to stay first."

"Don't worry," Lai said. "We are not sure in any way if they will take us both."

I was worried and fearful of the unknown. I tried to steady my breath and calm the fear that had become a tangible, living force creeping over me like some hungry beast, immobilizing me, holding me captive. My face went blank.

"Come on," Lai said. "We can do this."

Immediately, I decided to put a stop to my fearful thoughts so I could pay close attention to the upcoming interview. I decided to claim my power and take responsibility to be calm and in control because I realized that was the only road to peace.

The interview, together with letters of recommendation from Guam Memorial Hospital, clinched our success. I received the good news well. "Wow, we were hired on the spot!" I told Luz on the phone. "We are the only Filipina nurses here."

"Congratulations! Well done!" Luz said. "Now we need to find a place for you to live. When do you start to work?"

"We told them we would be ready in three weeks. Hopefully, we can find a place to stay by then," I answered happily.

Unable to find a secure, desirable place for us to rent, Luz decided to buy a house in San Francisco not far from work. In the meantime, we found a temporary place to live, a big Victorian house on Hayes Street. We didn't know it was a boarding care facility for the aged. The owner was very nice and catered to us as if we were her own children. A nursing home was something new to me. We didn't have many places like that in the Philippines or Guam. We took care of our elders at home.

I was curious to meet the people who lived there. I noticed one woman sitting all day in a chair by the window. In the bright spring daylight, her hair was snowy white. Her skin made her look like a wax dummy, and her fingers looked as if they were crudely carved with sharp tools. Her head was in constant motion as if she was agreeing with a sentiment no one else could hear, or perhaps she was listening to the ruminations of her mind, mulling over a lifetime that was drawing to a close. On her dresser were many photographs, including a black-and-white wedding portrait. The glowing bride stood tall and proud, holding a bouquet of newly opened roses, beside a man a head taller than she. When I looked at the white-haired woman sitting there in the room and then at the photograph of her youthful self, I understood why people call time a thief. Time steals so much so slowly until the last grain falls from our hourglasses and we are reclaimed by the Almighty. I learned so much in our short stay in that place about life and time. "Time slips away like grains of sand, never to return again," wrote author Robin Sharma.

Luz was able to buy a house on Forty-Second Avenue in the Sunset District of San Francisco. We loved the house. It had two bedrooms and was very close to our work. It was also only seven blocks from the same Pacific Ocean I came to know while living in the Philippines and Guam. I could feel the song in the walls of that house, and it raised my spirits in the quiet moments when the wind became still and the world seemed to pause to take a moment to breathe. In the silent words of that song, in the purity of its expression, I found my inner peace and realized that I was home. This house was clearly made with love.

At first, we took the bus to work, but after we had saved enough money, Lai and I bought a car. It was yellow, our favorite color. It was beautiful. And we liked that we didn't have to take the bus in the wee hours of the night.

We started to make friends there. It was the year the United States opened its ports to Filipino professionals who wanted to immigrate to the United States to work. We met most of them. Over time, we made many friends to travel with and simply enjoy. Fred had settled in Los Angeles, at the request of his sister, but he came to visit whenever he could. We always kept in touch with him.

We started to enjoy our life in foggy San Francisco with our newfound friends. We also enjoyed the visits of our friends from Guam, including Zeny Abatay, Sherry, and many others. Zeny, our classmate from PWU, had finished her two years in Texas and decided to stay with us. She started working at Kaiser Hospital in San Francisco, not too far from our hospital. Because we had only one car, we developed a schedule to help one another. I worked the seven-to-three shift, and Lai worked the three-to-eleven shift, the same as Zeny. So, Lai could take me to work at seven, take the car home to use, bring Zeny to work for her shift at three when I was finished, and then I took it home and picked them up at eleven. The schedule worked so well, we did it every workday.

It was a sunny day; the sunshine was in our bones. It was as if people glowed, their auras so happy on these summer days. Summer winds moved the lush foliage, creating an ever-changing mosaic of light and shade, and with it, the music born of such gentle movement, a steady, soothing lyric of nature, was melody and chorus all in one. It was beautiful.

I was in the midst of this beautiful reflection as Lai was driving our beautiful new car when I decided to put on my lipstick. For some reason, it fell on the floor. I looked down to pick it up as Lai was still trying to keep her eyes on the road, but then she tried to help me find it on the front-seat mat. She was distracted, and suddenly there was a loud bang. My head hit the windshield. The car had hit something. Everything stopped. Darkness. Ambulance siren . . .

One moment, the road was there, wide open and safe; the next moment, there was a loud noise, an acrid smell, and a pain that I may never recover from. A car crash comes as a shock, an aspect the movies and novels are not good at showing. It is the equivalent of looking without seeing, a form of emotional blindness.

"Don't take me to a nursing home!" I shouted as I was being put on a gurney. "No, no, not the nursing home!" I heard someone say, "She hit her head on the windshield — badly." I kept my eyes closed. Nothing seemed to make sense. "The other one is okay, only a bleeding lip." The voices faded as my brain tried to stay awake. *Do not sleep. Do not sleep. I need to stay awake.*

I woke up at Trinity Hospital. Lai was admitted for observation and was in my room getting ready to leave. I lay in bed unable to ignore sickening nausea and a headache. I just didn't feel well. Everything around me was spinning as though I were permanently tied to an ever-moving roller coaster. I tried to get up, only to learn that my legs were numb. Everything in the room was moving in a circular motion. Everything was coming in and out of focus. "Lai, what is happening? I am so dizzy. I cannot even stand up."

"I'll call the nurse," she said.

The nurse hurried in and tried to calm me down. "Honey, the doctor is coming. You banged your head pretty hard. The doctor will talk to you about your care. In the meantime, do not get out of bed until we figure out what is happening. Here, hold on to the call button. Press this if you need anything, okay?" she said as she fixed my cover.

"Okay," I answered.

A very nice-looking older doctor came in. "Hi, Thelma. I am the doctor in charge of your care. You hit your head hard on the windshield of your car when it hit a light post. How are you feeling? Do you remember anything that happened?"

"Not all of it, Doctor," I answered. The good doctor pulled up a chair and explained what had happened to me. Holding my hand, he said, "You suffered a severe concussion of your brain. The signs and symptoms you might be experiencing — like headache, ringing in the ears, nausea, vomiting, confusion, feeling like you are in a fog, amnesia surrounding the event, and constant dizziness — are among the many symptoms of the trauma you had. The numbness of your legs is uncommon, and I will have to carefully watch that. I am going to put you on complete bed rest — I mean *complete* bed rest. You cannot get up to go to the bathroom. You need to stay completely in bed without raising your head. I do not want to scare you, but you need to know that there is a possibility that you could be paralyzed for life if you do not follow these instructions. It might happen now or maybe twenty years from now if you don't cooperate. Do you understand what I am saying?"

"Yes, Doctor," I answered as sadness overcame me and tears flooded my eyes.

"I will be here to take care of you, but you need to help yourself," the doctor continued. "I need your complete understanding and cooperation. I will talk to your sister in my office as soon as she arrives. She told me that she is on her way."

"Okay, Doctor," I said.

After he left my room, anxiety set in. The thought of the possibility of my being confined to a wheelchair my whole life was horrible, not only for me but for my whole family, most especially my inay and itay, who hoped to see me always vibrant and healthy. I became full of fear. I could feel my heart rate increase, and my muscles trembled. I became sweaty yet had chills. I could not go home if I couldn't walk. I would have rather died than subject my parents to the heartache of seeing me in a wheelchair all my life. I didn't understand why this happened. What did I do wrong to suffer like this? I could not stop feeling dizzy. What was happening to me?

Ate Remy found me in this desperate condition and said, "Tem, keep your faith. You will recover. I will come here every day to be with you to help take care of you."

Soon after, I found out that my sister could not drive the forty miles to San Francisco without taking Valium; she now had such a fear of driving. I love my sister. She proved that nothing could hinder her from coming to help me. She conquered her fear because she loved me.

Panic attacks occur when the brain keeps sending messages of fear to the upper brain. Thoughts become scattered so that normal functioning is impossible. That is the reason why a person who is loving, kind, and calm can have such a powerful healing effect on someone suffering from this kind of injury. Their steady love feels medicinal. For someone to say, "I am here for you," slows the messages of fear. For someone to say, "You are safe and protected," also slows these messages. It gives the higher brain a chance to become focused and functional once more.

My sister coming every day and my friends' support mentally put me back in the driver's seat and started me on the road to recovery from my accident — a slow but sure recovery. I had to take two months off from work to completely recover. I am so grateful to my friends and family for their support and for restoring my faith in God and in myself.

CHAPTER 20

I Meet Florendo

Meeting you was not the first day of the rest of my life;
It was the first day of my life.

— *Steve Maraboli*

IT WAS A GOOD DAY. The ward was not as busy as the day before. I had time to look out the window of the hospital at the world outside. The view of the Golden Gate Bridge was breathtaking, as if I were in a fairytale. The velvety clouds were dancing around the sun. It was a beautiful sight. A mild breeze whispered through the trees. "Tonight will be beautiful," I said to myself. "We are going dancing at the Fairmont Hotel!"

The Fairmont Hotel is a very historic and luxurious hotel in the wealthy San Francisco neighborhood of Nob Hill. Lai and I were invited to attend one of our friends' birthday celebrations in the hotel's Tonga Room, which was known for its unique tropical décor — including an artificial lagoon! We could bring guests, too, so we were very excited.

Lai and I decided to get our beauty rest right after we got home from work. It was only three in the afternoon, so we had time. We asked Zeny to wake us at six.

I was in a deep slumber when I heard Zeny say, "Tem, Lai, it's time to get up."

"Thank you," I said. I was so excited and felt my heart skip a beat when I thought of going to the Tonga Room, to such a beautiful place, and there would be dancing.

I put on my black dress and paired it with my pearl necklace. I decided to wear my long hair down; it fell to my waist. I went to the mirror to put on my makeup. I have fair skin, so just a slight dusting of powder made my skin look like porcelain — flawless and youthful. The little touch of eye makeup I applied made my brown, almond-shaped eyes look bright. For shoes, I chose to wear my red, two-inch heels. "I think I am ready to go to this place of grandeur," I said to myself.

I was still putting some finishing touches on my hair when I heard Zeny call, "Tem, are you ready? Kuya Tony is here with some new friends." Kuya Tony was our friend who was like a brother to us, and because he was older, we called him Kuya. "They want to meet you and Lai."

"I will be there," Lai said and went to meet the newcomers.

I could hear laughter coming from the living room as I finished fixing my hair. "All right, here I come, ready or not," I said to myself as I rushed to the living room with a cheerful smile. Four gentlemen got up to greet me, and Kuya Tony said, "Tem, meet your new friends."

"Hi, my name is Ser."

"Hi, my name is Jun."

"Hello. Nice to meet you both," I said graciously. "My name is Thelma."

I turned to greet the other one, who seemed to be looking at me as if he was looking at a ghost. He took a big breath and said, "Hi, I am Flor."

"Hi, I am Thelma," I said with a smile. I wondered, *What is up with this guy? He seemed to be deep in thought for a moment there.* I put that thought aside and invited them all to the party.

The bright sun adorns the sky as if she has some bright ideas, something brilliant that needs to shine upon the Earth; the moon is a warm, pearly glow as if a simple glimpse of it can bless the eyes of anyone willing to look up to see it. Sitting next to a window in the beautiful Tonga Room, I looked up, and

I saw the great moon soaked in the light of the sun. The moon was even more beautiful than the stars around it.

I was deep in my thoughts when I heard Flor ask gently, "So, when did you come to America?"

"Oh, we arrived in the USA in June 1968 from Guam. I came with Lai and our best friend, Fred, to see and explore the world."

"When did you leave the Philippines?" he asked. "Have you ever worked in the Philippines?"

"Oh, yes," I answered. "I worked in Lipa City as an intern at San Sebastian Hospital. I left in May of 1965. I lived in Manila and worked as a private duty nurse until I left for Guam in June 1966. We stayed in Guam for two years and then moved to the USA in June 1968."

"Did you like Guam?"

"Oh, yes. I really enjoyed my stay there," I casually answered. He seemed to want to keep talking, but Lai wanted us to join everybody on the dance floor, so we did.

Flor was a very good dancer, full of energy and enthusiasm. His joyous, merry laugh was contagious. This man in a brown coat and eyeglasses was a well-oiled machine on the dance floor. He did not dance to be flashy or to make the girls watch him, but they did. He danced as if dancing was an art that revealed his happy soul. He sang too. He was the kind of singer who had a way of scorching the sins of the world and showing me that I was all right and born to love and be loved. That night, we danced the night away until both of us could no longer feel our legs. We danced so much that I found out just how strong I was as I was able to dance all night in heels! That night was the start of a beautiful friendship, a friendship that made us both more complete.

No outward attribute of Flor's made him a handsome man, though his eyes came close. From his eyes came strength, tenderness, and compassion. Maybe that is what a gentleman is — not someone who is dangerously weak or irritatingly polite but someone of great spirit and noble ways. This was who he was. What was beautiful about him came from deep within. No, he was not that handsome on the outside, but inside he was beautiful. I knew I would keep him as a friend forever.

Flor became my best friend. He had the gentlest soul but was also my defender, my protector from all storms. He became the one who held my soul as if it were new and placed a warm blanket over it to keep me safe. He became my sun so that there was always light in my world. When the night seemed so dark it was perfectly black, Flor's friendship was the light inside my soul that grew brighter and radiated out through my eyes. That was what a best friend could do. I realized that with Flor as my best friend, I was more blessed than ever.

Flor listened to me as if my words were as bright as gold. His responses told me he thought deeply about what I said. His words were always kind and helpful. His concern was so immediate that, for him, it seemed natural. He was devotedly thoughtful, an attractive feature I had not seen in a man for quite some time. A man who would take your entire spirit as his friend and always keep it safe, he could sense someone's life's story. His attractiveness, his charm, came from his soul, which shone through his eyes and revealed itself in the ways he expressed himself and in the song in his voice. I saw in him a conviction that he had the ability to endure.

When Flor walked into my life, I thought he must have been looking for someone other than me. Yet, it eventually became apparent that our meeting and friendship were destiny. Fate took control to give us a chance to be the very best of friends we could ever be — a chance to see the painting on the canvas of our souls, a painting of many colors and rising hope.

He brings to mind this observation by First Lady Eleanor Roosevelt: "Many people will walk in and out of your life, but only true friends will leave footprints on your heart." His prints were all over mine.

CHAPTER 21

Finding Love in Foggy San Francisco

If I know what love is, it is because of you.

— *Hermann Hesse*

Views of the Pacific Ocean and San Francisco Bay are often veiled in fog, which seems to have inspired the imagination of the people who founded the city and gave it an aura of romance, adventure, mystery, and lofty ideals. The "forty-niners" who came during the 1849 Gold Rush, the writers of the Beat Generation, the hippies of the Summer of Love in 1967, and the large gay and lesbian population have all contributed to San Francisco's aura of tolerance and romance. Daydreamers there are not merely inspired by rainbows; they become rainbows. They become the beautiful flowers they imagine growing in abundant generosity all over the Earth. They become the raindrops that descend with joy. They become the gold at the end of the rainbow. Creativity brings dreams to life — inspiring, enchanting dreams — leading them closer to the divine.

That vibration of creativity and joy followed us to our house on Forty-Second Avenue. My housemates — Lai, Zeny, Letty, Mameng, Ruby, Mayet,

Diana, Joy, my niece Lilibeth, and our friend Cynthia — became my family, my soul sisters. Our house became a home, a place of community, a place to laugh, to come together and have fun with old and newfound friends.

Real and beautiful friendships were forged in our house. It became a place where we built memories that would last for a lifetime. We danced every day and sang every day as we tackled life's joys as well as life's challenges. We became each other's protectors and defenders as well as each other's teachers. We watched each other grow from mere caterpillars into butterflies, free to fly to find nectar in every flower's bloom. We were grateful for each other.

In this house, strangers became family. We became a source of support and refuge for many newly arrived professionals from the Philippines. We were eager to help. We all had once been in the same situation, so it was a pay-it-forward gesture, I suppose. We found the greatest friends among them, and I am so grateful.

We met many friends as we traveled about this foggy San Francisco. Like Rey, a gentleman who inspired us and taught us different ways to make life enjoyable. Charlie was a handsome, spirited fellow who taught us the value of every cent by counting every orange in front of our very eyes and dividing them equally for our benefit. Joey was another likable guy who taught us the power of compound interest, which I still benefit from. They were all accountants who tried to teach us to manage our money well. They taught us how to buy in bulk to save money. Charlie would help us buy in bulk and show us how we could save money by sharing the goods

My friends and I also traveled around California as one family. We picnicked in Vallejo, visited Lake Tahoe, and picked grapes in Stockton. They even went with me to meet my parents when they arrived in the States. All trips to remember. Everywhere we went, we always had laughter and joy to bind us together as one. Our incredible friendship was based on trust and respect for each other, a friendship that would help us on our journeys through life. Through my friends, I learned to choose to feel my feelings, not to deny my humanity but to embrace it.

I watched as evening sunbeams cast extensive shadows on the ground. The oblique glimmer of the setting sun added a fervent, coral tinge to the cloudless sky, enough to bring a sense of calm. The colorful sunset was like a powerful melody that became more emotional, vibrant, and beautiful as the sun sank to the horizon. The sun going down reminded me of a good friend waving goodbye. He was leaving, but I knew deep in my heart that I would see him again.

That was how I felt about Flor. He left me every evening but came back every day when he had finished work. He and Jun had just moved to the Sunset District to be near us. Our friendship began to flourish like a summer flower and became a harbor from any storm. Flor was somebody who believed in me. He was the cradle for my humble spirit, the very fabric that kept me warm. I am grateful to the universe and every star above that helped us make our way together. My life changed. I was free in Flor's presence — in the bliss of his smile, in his companionship.

I have learned so much about the meaning of true friendship. The definition of a true friend is someone who has your back no matter what, watches out for you, and ensures that you are free from danger. A true friend will always have your best interests at heart. A true friend loves you unconditionally, supports you, encourages you to do better, and trusts you with absolute confidence. They are selfless. They are not judgmental; they are your ally.

The friendship that Flor and I developed as the days went by became the backbone of our relationship. It fed my soul. I was so happy with Flor's friendship that I tried to pair him up with my friend Cora, hoping that he would be more comfortable being in love with someone I imagined to be the girl of his dreams.

"Flor, my friend, you should find time for Cora. She is such a nice girl," I would say to him. Every time Cora was around, he would look at me and smile.

Our relationship continued to grow in strength and power, which helped us learn how to be better friends. We became each other's support. We learned to trust each other with respect.

The night was velvety dark but for the light of the bright stars, maybe serving as an assurance that even when we wish for the sunlight, there are stars to convey the hope of dawn. It was a beautiful night to attend a party with our coworkers from the hospital — our secretary, doctors, and nurses. Most of our friends would also be there. It would be a grand ole party.

I wore my yellow dress, white shoes, and a white sweater. Lai wore the gorgeous blue-and-white dress she had bought at Macy's. We both looked beautiful, and we were excited. Lai was driving our newly purchased yellow car, and we thought we were pretty cool. The vehicle appeared to be infused with the spirit of the night, so Lai's driving was naturally pleasant and delightful. We pulled into the parking lot and could already hear the music coming from the party house nearby. We eagerly jumped out of the car and slammed the door. "Oh no," I heard Lai say. "I left the car key in the ignition!"

I looked inside the car. "Uh-oh. The engine is still running."

Lai, panicking, asked, "What time is it?"

I looked at my watch and said, "It's almost eight."

"Who do you think can come and help us at this hour?"

I paused for a moment and said, "Maybe I can call Flor to come help. It's Saturday, so I hope he's home. The only thing is, I don't know his number. I never call him; he always calls me."

"Don't worry, I know it," Lai said.

A phone booth was just across the street. She gave me some coins and Flor's phone number. I walked across the street to call him and prayed that he would be home as I dropped the coins into the phone's coin slots. I dialed his number. "Hello?" I heard.

"Hello, this is Thelma. Are you awake?"

"Yes," he said eagerly. "I am still awake."

"I wonder if you can help us. We left the key inside the car, and the motor is still running."

"Okay," he said excitedly. "Please give me the address, and I will be there as soon as I can."

"Thank you so much," I said gratefully.

The night was cold but beautiful as the moon ascended, delivering a starry night sky. A large group of stars with dull eyes scattered around the moon. They were like beautiful flowers, sparkling beacons, lying quietly in black and blue. They seemed to grasp the moon; the moon was not lonely tonight.

Flor came to help us, and I can't explain why, but I suddenly realized that I couldn't leave him alone while he worked so diligently to retrieve the key inside our car. I bore with him the coldness of the night until he had succeeded. We invited him to go to the party with us. And he came. And we had a great time.

I rode home with Flor as Lai took our car to drop off some of our friends at their houses. He was so quiet, which was unusual for him. I kept my mouth shut too. *Maybe he is tired tonight,* I thought.

"Can we stop by my house?" he asked. "I just want to pick up something. I will be quick."

"Okay," I said. "I'll wait in the car."

When we got to his place, he ran in, came out with a package, and put it in the trunk of the car. He remained very quiet as he drove to my house. *I wonder what is bothering him,* I thought. I entertained myself by looking at the moon. She was such a welcome sight. I thought about how she appears like magic at each sunset and promises to return as she fades at dawn's first light. I thought about those faraway stars and how they returned each time shadows blend into darkness.

I was in this state of meditation when I heard Flor say, "We are here."

"Oh, good. Thank you so much."

"May I stay a little while?"

"Okay. Please come in."

I was glad we were home; he could relax. Our home was a happy and comfortable place. It was late, so everyone was asleep. I invited him to sit in the living room. He sat down with this huge bundle of something in his hands. He was still not talking, but I noticed something different in how he moved and looked at me, almost as if he were in a trance. His eyes were fixed on me, and he gave me a look of longing, desire, intrigue, passion, and, inevitably, a look of love. I did not know what was happening. Everything seemed to be moving in slow motion. Our conversation flowed as if we had known each other for years.

Flor handed me the huge package he had brought with him. It was a beautiful painting. He gently held my hand, looked into my eyes, and gave me his undivided attention. "I made this painting for you," he said. "I was remembering you in every stroke and in every color. You see, my dear, everything in me is connected to you. I dream of you. You have truly inspired me every day since the moment I first met you. You inspire me to follow my dreams and to be a better person. Tonight, I give you this painting as an expression of my true love for you now and always. It is a work of love. Although it may not be nicely done, it is lovingly given."

"Wow! Thank you so much. You painted this for me? It is beautiful!" I said with great excitement.

That beautiful painting birthed a new story. The story will be remembered by anybody who, by chance, sees Flor's painting, framed by memories of our love. The story behind the painting is a tale that needn't be told because it would be recognized by anyone. It began that very night, once upon a time, that truly starry night on May 17, 1970 — that one night when the sky was filled with swirling clouds, glowing stars, and a brilliant arched moon, marking the beginning of a new chapter in the book of our lives.

The transition from being the best of friends to lovers was not easy. The first few days were spent just trying to get a feel for each other. Flor's insecurity seemed to overtake him, and he became deeply despondent. Being a novice to this new and exciting relationship, I did not know how to help him except to be patient.

We talked over the phone for hours, and those conversations became the foundation for our relationship. We each laid out our principles along certain lines, and we tried so hard to make our lines congruent enough for takeoff. We learned to compromise and sacrifice for the good of each other. We came to realize the importance of good communication. Our struggle at this point in our relationship made us stronger. We realized that our love could weather any storm. We learned to extend to one another understanding and endless love. We made a solemn promise to possess our love until the end of time, and we made the Lord the center of that love.

One day, as we were walking in the park, Flor said, "Honey, I am so sorry for the trouble I gave you these past days. I know I wanted to change you according to my specifications. I was wrong, and I am glad you understand that I love you so much. I am so happy you have given our love a chance to bloom and grow. I know I have been so jealous, like a child. I felt so alone, like a child drowning in despair. I need you more than ever because I know you are the only one who can understand me. Please forgive me for being so desperately in love with you and being so demanding. I became so insecure and just want you only for myself. I forgot that you have your own personality, and I just have to accept you as you accepted me as I am.

"Thank you for giving me a chance to improve myself. Thank you for your continued support, for making me a better person when I am with you. I don't know how I can adequately communicate how much I love you. I want you to know that I am a better, stronger, humbler, kinder, and more grateful person through your love. The kindness and grace you show me every day help me live a better life with grace and dignity. Through your eyes, I find fantastic comfort. When you take my hand and squeeze it, I know all will be alright.

"You are my love, a constant reminder that life is worth living and love is worth giving. Our passion makes this world a magical place to live in. My beloved, you changed my life. You are an angel sent from above to make me a better person. Your beautiful smile can dispel all of my fears and insecurities. I can return to my faith and make life into a beautiful dream. In you, I have found what I have been looking for for so long. Please forgive me for being so hard on you.

"Beloved, I will never have the words to express all of my feelings for you. I am madly in love with you. My love will be forever yours. You are my diamond, my rock, a gem above all others. The light that shines from your eyes enlightens my soul."

He held my hand as we sat on the bench, and he looked into my eyes so tenderly, holding my gaze, touching my heart and soul to the core.

I looked at him with so much love, love that I had not felt before, and said, with teary eyes full of affection, "Honey, if you are wondering how much I love you, think no more, my love. You are the light in the heavens that streams into my essence, and I love you in every breath I take.

"My love, did you know that before I met you, I had never really been in love? I never believed it was possible to love someone so deeply and completely. Yes, some men had attracted me more than others, and they were so different from each other. You are the blend of all of them. You are unique in this world. So, I am so fortunate to have met you. I am frightened of such ecstasy and such agony, but your presence in my life has given me confidence that genuine passion really does exist. Because I share it with you. I have never wanted eternity until now; I never saw the point. But with you, I am courageous enough to let you take my hand and take a stroll in the park with me." I held his hand tightly and with so much love.

Angelita Lim wrote: "I saw that you were perfect, and so I loved you. Then I saw that you were not perfect, and I loved you even more."

CHAPTER 22

Love and Marriage

One life filled with great love is worth more than eternity.

— Anonymous

THIS NEW RELATIONSHIP, BASED ON true love and with God at the center, was like a new day, a fresh start, a clean slate. All of our carefully considered dreams were realized because we worked to make them happen. We were free to be ourselves. I was released to be me in this relationship, and Flor was liberated to be himself. Flor saw all of me, and I saw all of him. Flor accepted me as I was, and I accepted him as he was. There was so much independence in that, yet a strong sense of being home, of being liked, of wanting to stay forever. That became the secret of our strong bond and how it formed so fast.

Pure hearts can do that; that is the way love is. In this kind of love, whoever is significant to Flor is significant to me. Whomever Flor loves, I love too, and vice-versa. This new connection was coming together and forming a family — Flor and I. Sincerity became our water; our most profound devotion and true love became our sun. If we kept going the way our relationship started, our love would forever be fresh and evergreen.

Through this great relationship, we continued to make memories to last a lifetime. It all started with dancing at the Fairmont Hotel and then on to a cozy night club called Alexis, with friends getting together to seek joy and music in the middle of that night when the stars filled the sky like a pastel maze. Then there was the night Flor gave me his first love note, written on a small white napkin, a truly loving message. It was beautiful. It was a promise of light in the darkness that gave me a sense of blessed comfort amid the icy cold. The glittering cluster of stars of the night, as they have for thousands of years, beheld with eagle eyes this tiny moment of love.

We also shared memories across the bay in Sausalito, dining at a restaurant called Zack's, and had an incredible time listening to bongos and watching psychedelic lights flashing in Oakland's Jack London Square, and dancing the night away to Tina Turner's "Rolling on the River" at the Zanzibar. These joyous occasions made our relationship grow stronger. The picnic in Vallejo and our trips to Lake Tahoe, Stockton, and Hearst Castle would remain in our hearts forever.

Christmas Day came, more than a year after we first met. The bells tolled, and Christmas songs floated in the air, reminding everyone of the birth of Christ. Even before my eyes had let in the light of day, I could hear the bells from the neighboring church. Before us was a day of quiet contemplation, a day of thinking of the year ahead and how to bring Christ's love to humanity more than I had done the year before. Flor reminded me of last Christmas when I was trying to match him up with Cora.

"Honey, why were you trying to pair me with somebody else?" he asked.

"I don't know. Now I think I will keep you for myself, just because," I teased.

"You know that tomorrow I will be going on vacation with the rest of our friends. I really hope you can come with me," he said.

"Sorry, honey, I have to work," I answered.

"I know," he said. He held my hand and whispered in my ear, "I will miss you, my beloved, because of how I feel when I am with you. You are the last dream of my soul."

He left for Mexico that afternoon, but he made more phone calls to me than there were places he visited. He told me in one call: "Honey, to be honest,

I spend more time thinking of you than I do thinking about the places I go. My phone bills can prove it. You should know by now how much I am missing you during this trip. Believe me when I say that even though we are apart, you're still holding all of my heart."

"I miss you too," I replied. I realized that his absence had not taught me how to be alone but showed me that when we were together we created a pretty silhouette on an empty wall.

The day was July 17, 1970. My birthday. Flor invited me to celebrate it with him. He called me at work and said, "Honey, I would like to invite you out for your birthday tonight. Would you please wear the nice, red dress I gave you? I want you to have fun. I know that last year you were in the hospital because of your car accident. I wish you the greatest birthday today."

"Oh, thank you so much, honey," I said. "What time will you pick me up?"

"About six-thirty. Is that okay?"

"I should be ready by then."

The sun was setting over the horizon. Twilight was coming. I started to get ready for that night's celebration. This time, I wore my two-inch, red heels with my simple, knee-length, red dress. I again wore my pearl necklace and this time added pearl earrings. I put a little touch of makeup on my face and let my long hair fall to my waist. I felt that I looked stunning.

As I peeked through the window, I saw the bright, crescent moonrise and with it a starry night sky. Countless clouds gauzed the moonlight and seemed to hide a dreamland of elegant palaces. The night heavens, the bright moon and stars, inspired my innocent imagination. I thought it would be a great night.

The doorbell rang, and I thought, *It must be Flor. He is a punctual person.* I walked down the stairs. Flor was already inside; Zeny had opened the door for him. He was gazing at me with that fascinating look of love, which said much more than any words could express.

"Are you ready?" he asked.

"Yes, I am," I said as I waved goodbye to Zeny.

"Enjoy, you two," she said.

The night was beautiful, and we held hands as we walked in Jack London Square. The lights of San Francisco were sparkling across the bay. The crescent moon shone like a silvery hook in the sky. We were so happy as we looked up at the blanket of stars that stretched to eternity. It was a beautiful sight for two lovers trying to savor every moment.

Flor invited me to dine at the restaurant in the Waterfront Hotel in the Square, a place we had dined often with our friends. The hotel overlooked the bay, a beautiful sight, and its huge windows brought the outside in. There was something very intimate and relaxing about the place.

I looked around to take in the scenery and immerse myself in its incredible beauty. I observed the silvery-white moonlight sprinkled on the water and the stars playing with each other in the quiet night sky, each one stirring the sound of music within me. I was in this profound moment of reflection when Flor tenderly took my hand and gazed into my eyes with a tender look of love.

He handed me a gift. "Beloved," he said, "accept this gift on your birthday, a loving gift I have never offered anyone since my heart learned to beat. Marriage was written in my heart the day we met." As he slid a ring on my finger, he said, "It's not mankind or the law that makes marriage real, yet I know it exists because I know it was the universe that brought us together, for our souls were already betrothed. It is our destiny. I love you so much, and I want to love you forever. Please marry me."

I looked at him with sparkling eyes; my lifelong dream had come true. He looked like a plush bear in soft brown colors. His coat was kitten-soft, his smile a cup to hold safe my childhood desires, whatever they might be. I saw his warmth in his eyes. He was a perfect companion, the perfect one to hold, to nurture, to let the love energy flow.

At that moment in the garden in the mystical valley, I became the terrace and the walls, and Flor became the door and the key that opened my spirit. This mystical valley of emerald green set free my child self and invited me to join the infinite horizon of his soul. At that moment, I felt the greatness of real love, a real lover, and a true loving bond that would bring me a new strength and real peace. For real love is the most exquisite grace heaven can give. Real love is a champion, a guardian, a ride-or-die connection that stays with us always. It is raw, and it will holler for us if needed. It will stay with us in silence and be our solace. Real love will celebrate with us with joy and lift us up. It will accept our grief and protect the blemishes we hide from others.

It is truly rare — lifespan-rare. We need to cherish it and keep it as long as we live because it brings us stability and inner tranquility every time. There is no desire to change because, with real love, our true selves become one in love.

In that one great moment, I realized that we were one, no more he and I but *we*. So, I said, "Honey, I love you so much, and I know you love me too. Yes, I will marry you. In your arms, my storm is quiet; in your arms, I have peace; in your hands, I am home."

I saw the ring sparkle in the bright light. It was a simple diamond and looked like a bead of rain on the brilliant petals of a flower blossom. I saw the sincerity of what was blessed. Flor's heartfelt words suddenly became more extraordinary, more charming than this polished stone could ever be.

In our embrace, the world stopped still on its axis. There was no time, no wind, no rain. I was genuinely at peace. His love was pure, unselfish, undemanding. And free. I felt his body press in, solid and warm, and hugged him all the more tightly. *A love like this,* I thought, *I will cherish for life. Finally, I am home.*

At that moment, my whole life changed.

We began to plan for our wedding. Flor asked permission from my parents as well as my brothers and sisters to marry me. He showed me the letter he wrote to my mother:

Dear Inay,

I have been writing this letter for the past three days, yet I cannot choose the right words that I am trying to say. I feel speechless, not because there are no words on my lips but because of the overwhelming emotions.

Inay, before you left San Francisco, California, I was not quite sure if you had realized how much I love your daughter Thelma. These are the questions I ponder while I am writing this letter. I am sure that you would want me to love her with the same amount of love you have given her. I know you would like me to care for her the same unique way you do. I know you always want me to respect her the way people respect you. Inay, I learned these things because I love your daughter so much.

Because I love your daughter Thelma so dearly, I wish to convey my intention of marrying her as soon as you wish. I speak these words with confidence that I may be able to raise a family of my own. With God's guidance above all things, I honestly believe we will be able to carry on your dreams and ambitions for your children and our children someday.

I came from a family of poor people. My parents, who lived the life of poverty, are still working hard to get up once more from where they were, but fortune seems elusive. We are educated through hard labor and self-sacrifice, leaving nothing for us at the very end.

We have no wealth or property as a promise for tomorrow. I promise Thelma no wealth, for I have none, but I can give her all my love more than anything else. Inay, I am coming to you with open arms, longing for your embrace. I am coming to you as your child seeking your prayers.

Inay, I sent a letter to my father in Batangas, telling him of my intention. I gave him your address in San Juan, Rizal. He will contact you.

So long, Inay, and I am always wishing you the best of health. Will I expect a letter from you? So long for now.

Your son,
Florendo L. Villena

Preparing for our wedding was not easy. One of Flor's uncles thought we should not marry because Flor was poor and I was rich. I almost backed out. I felt that if some relatives did not like me then the marriage would not work. Flor was able to convince me that everything would be all right, that our love for each other was enough to face the challenges that would come our way. He confessed that he saw me at San Sebastian Hospital in Lipa City in 1965. He said, "Every time I went to Lipa, I watched you at the hospital. I decided to introduce myself, but it was too late. You were gone by then."

"Why did you not tell me before?" I asked.

"I was so afraid that you might think that I was stalking you, so I kept it to myself," he said.

"Did you recognize me when I saw you the first time?" I asked.

"Yes, but I needed to be sure. Can't you see, honey? We were destined to be together. I never thought I could see you again, but the heavens above led me to you three weeks after I arrived in the U.S. Can't you see, honey? God must want us to be together," he insisted. In the end, love wins. We decided to go against all odds with the promise to love each other no matter what life brought us.

Flor wanted to have a big wedding, but I refused because I knew that he needed help to bring his family from the Philippines. The wedding would be a small gathering of close friends and family with a reception at Joe's of Westlake, an Italian restaurant in Daly City. Unpretentious and small but unforgettable. Flor made a vow to have a bigger reception on our twenty-fifth anniversary.

Flor decided that he wanted to buy a house before the wedding. He worked every night to save money by selling Cutco pots and pans after he put in a full day at his regular job for an international engineering company. He said that we could host the reception at the house instead of paying for a place that would cost us about four hundred dollars. He worked hard every day to save for a down payment for the dream house. I supported him by making sure he ate right and slept right. He was able to buy the house with a five-hundred-dollar down payment and the help of the previous owner of the house, who allowed him to borrow the down payment and pay it back in monthly installments. Flor taught me through that experience that if you truly want something you can do it as long as you have desire, purpose, and stamina — and the Lord's guidance.

Our wedding day finally arrived — December 18, 1971. There was a sense of serenity on this perfect day, a peace that invited itself into our souls. The blue sky brought harmony to my steps, a composition with a constant tempo to complement the birdsong. The blue sky, a perfect dome of protection, played music with the sunlight on this fine day, a symphony of laughter that encouraged our creative souls to rise, to dream, to love and be loved, to fly. Over the years the depth of our love became as deep as that blue sky, and only we perceived the power of its protection. Our dreams coming true mirrored the blue sky of fairytale dreams to hold and behold forever.

St. Gabriel Church in San Francisco was beautifully decorated with white and purple flowers surrounding the altar. A red carpet was beautifully placed as a pathway for the bride as she made her way down the aisle to meet her groom. I felt beautiful in the gown my mother made for me. It was embroidered with pearl beads and rhinestones, and its long train flowed behind me on that red carpet. I wore a white veil with a matching headpiece, and in my hand I held a white orchid with a little touch of purple.

The church door opened, and I walked through it, and the love song from the movie *Romeo and Juliet* played. I felt like I was floating. Holding my father's arm, I walked slowly to the altar. I couldn't help but smile at my soon-to-be husband. He never looked so handsome as he did then in his white barong tagalog and black pants. My heart leapt with joy, and sunshine flooded my soul. I looked at Flor. He smiled. He was glowing with happiness. He was bursting with joy, and his spirit was bright. Happiness ran through our souls like warm ocean waves and washed away all the doubts we had had about this day. At that moment, we both knew that our marriage was truly a match made in heaven.

CHAPTER 23

Blessings of Marriage

No relationship is all sunshine,
but two people can share one umbrella
and survive the storm together.

— *Anonymous*

FLOR'S MOTHER ONCE SAID THAT Flor was a "diamond in the rough," and I knew what she meant. But to me, Flor was simply a diamond. He navigated through the world differently. The rest of us choose to be resilient to problems or not, but he was never beset by them. He radiated inner beauty no matter what. I guess that's why I fell in love with him. He had a light that nothing and nobody could ever steal. Flor was the most cherished treasure in my life. He was my one and only.

Our first year of marriage was full of personal conflicts and adjustments, but together we always found a way to bring peace to our home. We felt that special warmth, that wonderful feeling of love, which allows the winds of heaven to dance within us. We learned so much about being married — to let our love be like a moving sea between the shores of our souls. We tried to make our marriage full of laughter and joy, a place in paradise. We learned to sail through our adversities as one team. We became the best of friends as well as lovers.

Flor and I were sweethearts, so beautiful things happened to us. We both grew in all ways, and we began to flourish in ways we never realized possible. We each became a better version of ourselves yet were still ourselves. We loved each other very much, so we knew we were suitable for each other. We both strove to make a beautiful marriage with Love at the center of it all. That first year was the year our baby was born.

On September 11, 1972, the labor began. First, it felt like solid menstrual cramps that took my breath away, and I could hardly walk. As my labor continued, the pain became worse. Every time a contraction came, the muscles in my lower back slowly seized up, and they twisted harder and harder as the labor progressed. The pain grew more and more, so I asked Flor to take me to the hospital.

"Honey, I think I am ready to go to the hospital," I said.

"Okay, honey," he answered.

St. Mary's Hospital in Daly City was about fifteen minutes away from our house. Flor had been practicing driving there to make sure he made it on time.

"Hon, I will just go to the bathroom, and then we can go, okay? The pain is really severe this time."

"Okay," I heard him say.

I came out of the bathroom in a lot of pain. It was so intense that I could not talk. I looked for Flor. I could not find him anywhere. The pain was more intense now. I glanced up at the ceiling with tears flooding my eyes. "Where is Flor?" I cried. Fear overtook me, and I had a hard time breathing.

All of a sudden, Flor came running through the front door. "Oh, honey, I was so excited, I thought you were already in the car. Oh, my Lord, honey, I am so sorry! I went to the hospital, and when I opened the car door, you were not there! Please, please forgive me. I got so excited!"

I understood Flor's being shocked and feeling overwhelmed. I knew he was scared too. I wished I could have said more, but the pain was too severe. All I could do was bite my lower lip and sigh. "Let's go," I said and took his hand. He put his hand on my hip and gave me a gentle massage, which helped a little.

"I cannot believe I left you. I am so sorry," he said again.

Melissa was born on September 12, 1972, after thirteen hours of labor. The moment I laid eyes on our baby, I forgot those painful hours. I was aware of only the joy and jubilation our baby girl brought us. Flor couldn't hold back his tears of joy when he held Melissa for the first time. We were bowled over with joy. Flor's happiness streaked through him like a comet. Melissa was a gift sent from Heaven above. She brought us smiles, laughter, and love. That day marked a new beginning, wrote a new page, and crossed a new threshold in yet another episode of our lives. That day, we became a family of three, full of love and affection.

I was able to stay home from work longer than expected to care for the baby, having worked sixteen hours on the day before delivery. Flor was very much against my working a double shift, but I explained how much the hospital needed me. I loved him so much for understanding, and now I had that extra time to be with my new baby.

We watched Melissa grow into a beautiful baby girl, and every day our life was happy. She was indeed a bundle of joy. We watched her learn to crawl and then take her first step, a fascinating event. She liked to wear a fancy, yellow dress my mother made for her, and she wore it with a matching, yellow hat, which she adored, that set off her silky, black hair. She always wore her little, yellow dress with a big smile. Melissa made the experience of being parents for the first time a wonderful experience, one that we would remember as long as we lived. We thanked God for the blessing He had bestowed upon us. Our bond of love for each other grew every day. Our home became a beacon of hope and love.

We continued to be two lovers living our dreams and fantasies, wishfully planning and shaping our future, which was not easy. On the nights when Flor was so involved in his work that he couldn't come home, loneliness permeated my whole being. The sun continued to shine in the morning, and the moon still lit the sky above, but his absence made my days incomplete. Flor was a good partner, a blessing from above, who made me realize that life was hard, and we had to be prepared to negotiate challenging roads together. With every obstacle we faced, the love between us grew stronger, and we learned that love was, above all, willing to endure. It was our strength, which allowed us to carry on when storms set in. We learned that the most incredible legacy of love is not revealed in the sweetest jubilation but in the torment and agony of defeat, in the sacrifices for one another. Together, we learned that love wins when all else fails.

Flor's travels to Europe and the East Coast made his heart yearn for us more and more. We made our home a place of peace, tranquility, and love. Flor coming home from one of his trips was always a wonderful experience. Our house became his refuge, a haven where he could rest his feet and relax. We learned to communicate better and to set our priorities. We believed that life is a game in which we keep five balls in the air. The five balls are work, family, health, friends, and spirit. We learned that work, or a job, is a rubber ball. If we drop it, it will bounce back to us. The other four — family, health, friends, and spirit — are made of the most delicate glass. If we drop any one of them, it will break and shatter. We kept reminding ourselves that we couldn't have everything, but we already had what was essential — our family, friends, health, and a joyful spirit. We thanked God every day for these blessings.

In December 1974, two years after Melissa was born, I was eight months pregnant with our second baby, and we decided to go to Hawaii for our Christmas vacation. Melissa was so excited about her first plane ride.

We visited my sister Luz and my brother-in-law Angel on the Island of Oahu, the most populous of the eight islands that make up the state of Hawaii. The weather was fantastic — in the high seventies to low eighties — and the beaches were beautiful. We had a great time exploring all the interesting places there, including Pearl Harbor, bombed by the Japanese in 1941, and Honolulu, the state capital. It was a great vacation that we will never forget, thanks to the generosity of the Abcedes. This was a place we would always enjoy visiting.

On February 2, 1975, our life drastically changed again for the better. After fourteen hours of labor contractions, the pain quickly vanished, just as it had with Melissa, as soon as I held my baby boy. Flor rushed out of the delivery room with his spirits flying high to call my parents to announce that we had a boy. When he came back, he held the baby for the first time, staring with wonder at him. He never took his eyes off him. He could barely contain his happiness. I watched as his spirit brightened, and he again cried tears of joy, just as he had when Melissa was born. I realized how amazing a dad he was. The birth of his son made him the happiest man in the world, and that moment of gratitude flowed through my heart. I looked to the heavens above to say a prayer of thanksgiving, and quiet contentment spread through my whole being. He left the delivery room with his heart singing with over-whelming joy and a prayer of thanksgiving. "Thank God it's over," he said.

The birth of our baby boy, whom we named Florendo Garcia Villena, Jr. and called V.J., came at the same time Flor passed the California Board of Professional Engineers exam, and I passed the Civil Service Exam for the City of San Francisco. That allowed me to be a permanent employee of the City of San Francisco as a head nurse. We were moving forward profession-ally and financially, so we bought an apartment on Noriega Street in the city to have as a rental. We worked hard to put the place in order, painting the rooms, cleaning the kitchen. Though I didn't know how to do any of those things, I stood by my husband and gave him my support. "Honey," he said one day, "I know you are not used to this kind of labor, but I am glad you are with me, and I love you more and more for it. You are always with me in every way you can be, whether it's hard or sad or happy, and I love being with you. Thank you so much for always being there for me." I just smiled because I knew he truly loved me more and more.

Our marriage had become like a garden. It needed time to grow, but our love nurtured it every day. We came to understand that a rising number of couples were calling it quits; it seemed to be harder than ever to make a mar-riage last a lifetime. We found out that marriage takes work and commitment and love but also needed respect to be truly happy and successful. We started to water our relationship with clear, loving communication on a regular basis.

We were able to express affection through spoken words of praise and appreciation. This was Flor's primary communication of love. He loved writ-ing love notes to me every day, too, and called me at work at least once every day, sometimes more. I learned to practice this excellent gesture as well. We showed our love and appreciation to one another by talking to each other and using words of love and affection. We learned to give each other our undivided attention and additional quality time when we could. I discovered that this was important for our marriage. One day, I decided to learn to crochet. I was so focused on learning this new craft and the counting required that I became quiet for quite a while. Then one night, Flor said, "Honey, would you give me that needle?"

"Why?" I innocently asked. "Do you want to learn how to crochet?"

"No," he said. "I just miss you talking to me. I love to talk to you, you know."

I stood, gathered up my crochet hook and threads, and put them in a box, never to touch that box again. I looked at him through the eyes of love and held his hand. I said, "Honey, you are the best thing that ever happened to me. I love you so much."

He hugged me gently and said, "I love you forever."

We both learned to focus our attention on each other and to let love bind us together.

We found that physical affection was not necessarily about having sex. We showed appreciation by holding hands, sitting quietly together, holding one another in each other's arms, feeling so secure in each other's presence. Sometimes, Flor would sing the Frank Sinatra song, "The Nearness of You": "It's not the pale moon that excites me / That thrills and delights me, oh no / It's just the nearness of you." We helped each other in every task at hand and stood together to fulfill every responsibility. In one of his many letters, Flor wrote: "Dearest honey, thank you so much for always supporting me when I failed and was stumbling. You are always with me when I am happy or sad. I love you so much for always being with me."

We always remember to remain committed to each other, our family, and the life we built together. We support each other emotionally and in everyday ways. We are committed to communicating our undying love for each other and our appreciation for each other every day. *Together* has become our favorite place to be.

CHAPTER 24

The Mystery Letter

Life is a series of thousands of tiny miracles.
Notice them.

— Roald Dahl

OUR MARRIAGE BECAME STRONGER over time. We saw it as a big, beautiful portrait. Millions of brushstrokes and thousands of colors told our story of unending love and support, friendship, childhood dreams that came true, new discoveries about each other and life itself, sensual pleasures that had the fiery brilliance of a bright star, a marriage that had the tranquility of a sunset that brought the promise of a new dawn.

Having two babies had been relatively simple. Come summertime, we took our children — Melissa, who was four years old, and V.J., who was two-and-a-half — to Canada for a much-needed vacation. We were excited about traveling to new places. We visited Butchart Gardens in Victoria and found a lot of fresh fruits, such as lanzones, santols, and chicos, in Vancouver that I thought grew only in the Philippines. That was a pleasant surprise. We also visited the Space Needle in Seattle and an amusement park called Enchanted Forest in Oregon. It was a vacation we would cherish for a long time.

It was a day of jubilation in May 1976. Tatay and Nanay, Flor's parents, were arriving from the Philippines. Flor and I were so excited. It was my first time meeting them, and I was filled with joy. Flor was paralyzed with happiness. After all, this was his dream since he was a small boy. "Honey, what will I say to my father?" he asked nervously.

I smiled and said, "Just hug him. Remember, the heart speaks when no words come." He smiled. I knew that he was happy and that his spirit was flying high. This was just the start of the culmination of his dream. "Honey," he whispered, "soon we can get my brothers and sisters here too."

"Yes," I said and held his hands lovingly. The coming of Tatay and Nanay brought us so much happiness. We took them to our house in San Francisco.

Our dream of bringing Lannie, Charito, Neneth, and Jaime over became a reality in April 1977. It was a beautiful day. The weather was excellent. The sun was bright and refreshing after the "April showers that bring May flowers." Flor could not believe his eyes when he saw them; the last time he saw them was in September 1969 when he left the Philippines. "They are all grown," he said. "And they are finally here. One day, Jun, Eddie, and Vic, and eventually Tita's and Berting's families, will come here too. We will all be together again like once upon a time."

"Yes, you will be. Our dreams are coming true," I answered with a smile. "They are all beautiful, and Jaime is so cutely handsome." The minute I saw them, I knew they were my sisters and brothers in my heart. "I hope you will like it here. I love you all already," I said quietly to myself. The realization of our dreams brought contentment and joy to all of us.

We purchased a new home in Concord, California, on August 29, 1976. San Francisco schools were beginning the process of desegregation, and Melissa would have had a two-hour bus ride to school. So we bought a house in Concord and enrolled her in a public school there. That school announced sometime later that it was closing due to low enrollment, so we enrolled Melissa in St. Agnes School for the following year.

However, because St. Agnes was a private Catholic school, we had to tighten our belts. Together, we planned our budget, expenses, and projected savings, but things kept going wrong when we tried to implement our plan of action. Our car insurance went up, our heater broke, Flor's calculator malfunctioned, and our property insurance went up 39 percent. Our budget was out of balance, but we knew with faith and hope that tomorrow would bring brighter days.

"Arguments about money are by far the top predictor of divorce," says Sonya Britt, an assistant professor of family studies and human services and program director of personal financial planning at Kansas State University. "It's not the children, sex, in-laws, or anything else. It's money." Luckily for us, Flor and I had discussed money issues before we got married. Communication is the cornerstone of a successful marriage, and we listened to each other without interruption. We knew we needed to work together to solve the problems at hand. We understood that prioritizing and budgeting were important, and so was setting goals. We always sat down and discussed money issues with an open mind. We were able to handle our money well, so we did not put too much emphasis on it. We both believed that in our relationship no amount of money or success could take the place of time spent with our family.

It was a very special September night. Darkness came as strong, protective arms, holding us close until the promised dawn. I was thinking about work the next day and reminding myself to give my boss the leave of absence form I had filled out to prepare for my delivery date on October 5. I went to the bathroom to get ready for the night when I saw all the signs that I was going to deliver my baby sooner rather than later. "Honey, I think I am ready to deliver."

Flor got out of bed in a panic and said, "Honey, it's not October yet!"

"I know, honey, but all the signs are here."

Flor was quiet as he drove me to Seton Hospital in Daly City. I knew he was worried. Our beautiful daughter came earlier than expected — September 19, 1977 — but her birth marked the day of Flor's arrival in the United States in 1969. Flor was so excited to see her. He looked at her with so much love, just as he did when our other two children were born. He had the same teary eyes. It was a beautiful sight. I felt like I was falling in love with my husband all over again. At the same time as I was falling in love with my baby.

Our new daughter was a bundle of hope who stole our breath away and embraced our hearts. She was like a star in the sky, ready to shine. While she was in Flor's arms, she started to cry, and she was loud. "Wow, baby," he said. "I see you inherited my voice. You can sing. I will give you my song. Honey, we have a singer right here."

We went home after two days in the hospital. Melissa and V.J. were ready to greet their baby sister. They were both so excited! She was a gift, a blessing from Heaven. We named her Flordeliza, "lily flower," a combination of our names rolled into one. The presence of "Iza" in our life made us complete.

Iza's first birthday was a day to remember. I was getting ready for her birthday celebration when I found my itay unconscious in the bathroom. I tried to remain calm and called 911 immediately. My poor itay had just celebrated his ninetieth birthday in August. He passed away that day. I did not know how to feel. I had not lost anyone while I was growing up except for my favorite aunt when I was a student nurse. I could not believe my father was gone so quickly. The world seemed to stand still. Losing a father means losing a protector, a guiding hand, a superhero. I was speechless. I felt like I had a hole drilled into my heart. I couldn't imagine life without him. He was patient, kind, adventurous, loving, an anchor in life for all of his children. There was no end to my father's love. My itay was more than just a father; he was the soul of our family.

My mother had a tough time accepting his death. They had been married for fifty long years. Flor and I were grateful to have given them a memorable golden wedding anniversary celebration. My mother wanted to go home to the Philippines to try to forget, so after my father's funeral, she left to be with relatives there.

I was having a hard time without my father. In my anguish, the sunbeams wouldn't shine as bright, and the chirping of the birds simply passed me by as if their song couldn't glide through the air as it once did. Grief came in waves as if my soul needed to bleed an ocean through my eyes. Tears flowed endlessly. Flor, my beloved, stood by me, always loving, always understanding as he grieved with me. In those painful days of misery, he cared for me and consoled me. "I know your pain," he said. "Try to be strong. Listen to music, move, paint, enjoy the sunshine and the birds. Try to be happy. Remember and know I love you so very much."

My beloved husband listened to my grief and enveloped me in his tenderness just by his affectionate touch and compassionate words. He was my number-one supporter, my angel sent from above, and my hero. Everyone needs a husband like mine — a forever-increasing treasure of love and good feelings combined with an everlasting trove of experience when I did not know up from down. He was proud of me no matter what. He disregarded my failures and applauded my endeavors. He vowed to stand by me come what may, and he did. My husband was truly my best friend and lover, and I thanked God every day for the blessing. With my husband beside me, I could be happy once again. I could see the sunshine as a gift again, richly defining each moment as a cheerful, magical beacon of hope, surging skyward like the music of colors, bringing the passion of dance and songs to my bones.

Our life together was like a dream, a dream replete with jubilation and success as well as sorrow and disappointments. This was the time in our lives when we were together in sorrows and pain, happiness and joy. We both matured emotionally as we learned to respect, understand, and truly love each other more than ever.

We grew together as one but attained our professional goals as individuals. In September 1978, Flor was promoted to chief of the Control and Communication Department at the International Engineering Corporation in San Francisco, while I remained at San Francisco General Hospital as a head nurse. We both agreed that the kids were our priority, so I would not take any more promotions. Flor wanted me to quit working from the start, but I wanted to practice my profession for a while. He always reminded me about his promise to take care of me. Often he would say, "Honey, you should stop working so I can fulfill my promise to you that I will take care of you." I just smiled and said, "One day, honey. One day."

The kids were all in school, and Flor was busy with the demands of his job and our growing family. At this time in our life together, material possessions sometimes seemed to take on outsized importance. We began to believe that what we possessed and cherished on Earth were what we depended on to make us happy. We became spiritually forgetful. In the reality of life, we as Christians tend to drift at times in our faith journey. Although we are aware of the truth in the Scripture and know that it is central to our faith, in the press of daily life, we can forget this truth. We know that our lives have eternal significance and that we all face an eternal destiny, yet in the push and shove of our daily concerns, we are driven to focus on the "here and now."

This is what happened to Flor and me. The demands of life made us forgetful of our spiritual life. But God had not forgotten us. He sent us a minor miracle in the form of a forgotten note, a letter given to me by a nurse the day I had my car accident. I had forgotten this letter, but for some reason, it kept appearing. I showed the envelope to Flor and said, "Honey, this letter, which I have forgotten that I had, keeps showing up."

"Really? Did you open it yet?" Flor asked.

"No," I said. "It says, 'Open when you are ready.'"

"Ready for what?" Flor asked with curiosity.

"I don't know," I said. "Should I open It? I don't have any idea what it is. It is a very old letter from thirteen years ago. I don't even remember who gave it to me. I am very curious now."

"Maybe you inherited something," Flor said jokingly. "For all you know, this could be a miracle."

We decided to open the letter. It was dated July 17, 1968, and it said: "I know you don't know me. I have been praying for you since you were admitted to the hospital in July 1968. I hope when you open this letter you will be ready to learn about God's love through the Cursillo way. There is a Filipino Cursillo in San Francisco. Hope all is well with you. Your Sister in Christ."

We were both surprised. "Cursillo? I attended an American Cursillo twelve years ago," Flor said. "I had forgotten all about it."

Our close friends Joey and Cynthia Bautista were active in such an organization, so we contacted them and told them about the mystery letter. They were both very helpful and told us there was going to be a three-day Cursillo weekend coming up and that Cynthia was willing to sponsor me if I was ready. We said we would talk about it and then decide. Before Cynthia left that day, she said she believed that the letter showing up like that was a miracle. "Miracles are small things and are often for your eyes only," she said. "They are the summons the good universe dispatches, and you can expect them or not. I suggest that you let the gratitude in and find the courage to welcome it and believe."

That day, I came to believe in miracles, and the miracles I have witnessed with my own eyes and ears have been the confirmation I needed to trust that there is a Holy Spirit and an intelligent and divine universe that guides me with love. They are records with wings, remembrances with inner light, the kind that keep me honest in the core of who I am.

I decided to learn more about Cursillo before I joined the three-day weekend. The Cursillo movement is a Catholic-based training program that started in Majorca, Spain, in the 1940s and has subsequently grown world-wide. The full name, *Cursillos de Christianidad*, means "little courses in Christianity."

The three-day weekend began on Thursday evening and concluded on Sunday. It was intended to help practicing Christians renew and strengthen their love of Jesus and to learn how to bring that love into all aspects of their daily lives in very practical ways. For those three days, laypeople and clergy live and work together in order to become more aware of the value and responsibility of their faith. There was a series of spiritual talks and discussions that were both serious and lighthearted. The weekend was personal, lively, and informative, with singing, worship, and fellowship.

Joining the Cursillo changed the depth of our faith for the better in our lives. I made a commitment to live the Cursillo way, and Flor and I dedicated our lives to serving the Lord. Flor and I started to participate in the Cursillo movement, and our love for each other grew stronger every day. We found out that real faith and love with the Lord in our midst required the heart of a warrior, a true fighter, the kind of toughness that is filled with kindness. Real love, precious and lasting, became our holy grail. We sought that special kind of love that is very rare and binds eternally — that kind of heavenly love that brings peace and happiness every moment of every day.

In April 1984, Flor came home from serving on a team for a Cursillo weekend and looked a bit exhausted but excited and happy. He handed me a letter. It read:

My beloved,

I made my Cursillo twelve years ago in the same old Saint Benedict Center in San Francisco, not with the Filipino but with the American group. Perhaps I am one of the few Filipinos here in the Bay Area who is privileged and fortunate enough to enjoy the company of our American brothers. It is an experience I will always remember because, through them, I felt the love of Jesus. Through them, I found peace, as their prayers made me a new man.

I came out of the Cursillo with a mission deep in my heart to serve the Lord. I made a vow and a promise to continue to propagate the good news. My faith in Jesus gave me all the reason to hope for a better spiritual life in the days to come. I was able to sustain that promise for a few months, but after that, my priorities changed. Quite often, I needlessly made my profession, my job, my dreams, and my busy schedules the excuses for not seeking God.

Honey, you might not know this, but your decision to make the Cursillo after years of a beautiful marriage made me wonder why it took you so long to answer the call of Jesus. I realized I never asked you. Somehow the Heavenly Father took it upon Himself to call you to lead me to Him.

I know He uses you to bring me to love Him again. He called me through you, my beloved. He opened my heart that had been locked and lifeless for the last twelve years through you and through your love. Through you, I gained back my trust and faith. Because of you, I am alive again. I will love you forever.

Love,
Dad

After reading the letter, I looked at him and couldn't help but shed a tear. I felt his sincere love and affection. I said, "To be near you is like not being lonely. All of my life, I felt so deserted in a room without a window, a room with no doors. Then suddenly, you came as if you were walking over a golden pasture. How is it that you are significantly more than the rays of beautiful sunbeams? How can you inspire my soul when no other can? Why is it that you are my salvation? Who could care for me more than you? So, my love, I want you to know this: While I breathe, I am yours in mind, body, and spirit." I felt him brush my hair with his gentle touch, and he kissed me gently. No words because his heart spoke to my soul.

Flor's company needed him to fly to Africa that Monday, but I refused to let him go. He looked a little tired from serving at the Cursillo, and I wanted him to rest for a good while before the trip. He tried to convince me, but I did not let him go until the doctor gave him clearance to fly, and the doctor did. He promised to be back before the end of the month.

The day Flor left for Africa, the light of dawn seeped into our room. I rubbed my blurry eyes. I saw Flor sitting at the edge of the bed watching me sleep. This was not something new. He did this all the time as if he wanted to take my portrait with him. As I opened my eyes, I said, "Please stay," and I put my arms around him.

He looked at me with that look that took my breath away and said, "Honey, I love you so much. I will be back soon," and he gave me a gentle peck on the cheek. He did this all the time, but today it was different. At that moment, we could feel each other's breath, each other's soul. We became one in spirit. The rising sun cast a rosy hue on the two of us. We knew then that true lovers are never apart, maybe in distance but never in heart.

CHAPTER 25

That One Unforgettable, Awful Day

Your sudden loss was like a doubling of my life.
Now and forever after, everything I do is for both of us.

— *Kate Miller Wilson*

FLOR'S JOB IN AFRICA TOOK longer than expected, so he was unable to attend a three-day Cursillo with me. I could not do anything except pray for him all through the weekend.

I came home Sunday evening, tired but happy to be back with my children. It was a quiet night as the evening light cast long shadows on the ground. The distended rays of the setting sun gave the sky a warm orange glow tinged with red. The kids asked when their father was coming home.

"We miss him terribly," Melissa said, speaking for the three of them.

"Very soon," I said. "Very soon. His job is taking a little longer than we expected. As soon as his job is finished, he will be coming home for sure," I assured them. "Now, let's go to bed so we can have an early start for school tomorrow."

I could not sleep that night. I thought about my children. Melissa was getting tall. She was eleven years old, had beautiful black hair almost to her shoulders, a gorgeous oval face, and a charming smile. She was very responsible and did her homework without prompting. She wanted to be a nurse. She'd had that dream ever since she was four years old. She was the apple of her father's eye. When Melissa was about two years old, she was so cute and charming that she was invited to be in a commercial. But Flor was against the idea that his baby would "work" at that age. She always helped her younger siblings without being told. She had that caring characteristic even when she was very young and cared for her grandmother and grandfather. (My parents lived with us.) Truly a blessing from above. She was a little shy, though, so we signed her up to be a cheerleader.

V.J., Flor's only boy, was cute, playful, and creative. He liked sports, but he did not like school. He did not like having to sit still all day; he loved to move. He was not too tall, like his father, and liked to cry a lot for no reason. We spent restless nights thinking about him and his not liking school. He was now in the third grade.

Our youngest, Flordeliza, changed her name to Iza because she thought Flordeliza was too long. She was a healthy seven-year-old, and I liked her pretty eyes. Her personality was charming; she was very talkative and articulate. As Flor had predicted when she was born, she loved to sing, and she was good. Flor would say, "I gave her my songs."

Yes, they were our three children, born out of true love, blessed with hope for a good tomorrow, and showered with everlasting love. Flor and I spent countless hours thinking about how to care for them correctly. We knew we didn't have the power to design their futures, but we sure tried.

I drifted off to slumber with my children in my mind only to be awakened by what I thought was the sound of the garage door opening, as if someone was coming home unexpectedly at night. Suddenly, I felt a gentle, loving hug, so full of tenderness and affection. I felt an incredible feeling of overwhelming love that filled me with peace.

Signs from the universe can masquerade as a cradle song. They are a part of life. They get me from one day securely into the next day. Yet there are times when they overflow, when significant signs from the past weave together to warn of another blessing or another curse. The following day brought a downpour, a total overflow of signs. I couldn't tell what was to come, only that they were heralding extraordinary challenges. The result was unspoken, and I just had to believe that God was with me and to trust in the power of love.

The just-risen sun shone softly on the street, bringing with it a flurry of early-morning activity. I peeked out the window and saw an ambulance. "Hmm," I whispered. "What is an ambulance doing in front of our driveway?"

I changed clothes and ran downstairs. Two of Flor's coworkers, Damian Boncodin and Ding Victa, were talking to my inay. Damian stood up to tell me the news. "Tem, I am so sorry. Flor passed away this morning in Africa. We do not know all the details, but Flor must have suffered a massive heart attack. He was dead on arrival at the hospital."

I looked at him in disbelief. "This is not true. He promised he would come back."

I felt like my heart had been ripped out and split into pieces. I was in deep distress and could do nothing but bow my head and let the tears flow. I felt intense pain in my heart. I bit my lips to keep from crying. I sat silently, hunched over with a sense of loss so fierce that my muscles could not respond to any commands. That deep feeling of loss enveloped my whole being. "How could this happen?" I asked myself. "We did not even say goodbye." I glanced outside; that ambulance was still there. "Why is the ambulance here?" I curiously asked.

"Our office instructed us to order an ambulance because the president of the company is so concerned about you. The officers wanted to make sure you will be taken care of," Ding explained. I could not say anything. All I knew was that I had to save whatever strength I had for my children.

I felt so empty. I could not think, but so many thoughts were in my mind. Yet nothing made sense. My children, my children. What will happen to them? I needed to tell them but when? And how? Oh, my. What about Nanay and Tatay Villena losing their eldest son? Flor and I brought them all here to have a better life. How would my brothers- and sister-in-law feel? We brought them all here, but now Flor is gone? They would feel so fearful of the future. In my sorrowful heart, I knew I would always be there for them as they had been a part of me. I wanted very much to tell them, "Don't worry, Tatay and

Inay, I will always be here for you." But I was unable to speak. My mind was reeling. I did not know what to do. "Please, Lord, I need your help!" I cried. "I don't know if I can handle losing my beloved."

In that moment of loss, I journeyed through ripples of sorrow. In that most unpredictable of all emotional hurricanes, the pain of loss came to bear witness to the realness of true love. Because I truly loved him, I would have traded places with him in a heartbeat. "Lord, please take me, not him!" I cried in vain.

I found myself unable to breathe. I felt empty and hollow, with a constant ache in my heart. I had to lie down. My body, hands, and feet were freezing. I felt nauseated and had an unbearable headache. I could not open my eyes — they were too sensitive to light — so I lay in bed with my eyes closed. I never felt so sick and could not concentrate. I was unable to get out of bed. "Please, honey, help me with your kids," I pleaded.

It was almost time to pick up the children from school. The dappled sun shone through the trees, creating mysterious shadows. The blue sky was dotted with fluffy white clouds drifting lazily in the gentle breeze. My best friend, Lai, who had rushed to my side from Daly City, was there to drive me to St. Agnes. I used what little energy was left in my body to get up to pick up the kids.

Sister Rita Francis, a very compassionate nun who worked at the school, met me at the door. She gave me a big hug and said, "Remember, Thelma, God will never forsake you and your children. Hold on to His love, and understand that God loves you." Tears flooded my eyes, and I was unable to utter a single word. I gently hugged her back. Patting my back, she said, "I will pray for you and the children. I am always here if you need to talk." I nodded my head and left with my children to walk in the park.

After some time, I was finally able to open my mouth and tell my children that their beloved father was now in Heaven, and the hope of his coming home was an illusion. It was then that I gained a partial understanding of what it truly means to be a mother. I felt deeply the agony of my children's grief. I felt their pain and suffering and the fear in my heart, in the core of my being. I felt their shock, disbelief, and anxiety.

I realized then that being a mother is the most challenging job on Earth. My children were so young to be deprived of the joy of loving their father and being loved by him. My heart and soul ached for them. I was not prepared for this kind of loss, its effects and tribulations, but I knew I had to stand my ground to protect and support my children. I had to prepare myself to meet my children's demands as they experienced their grief. The profound misery I was feeling was not only mine but also my children's and my husband's — because I knew in my heart that Flor must have fought with all his might to stay with us.

At the moment I thought of Flor, Melissa shouted, "Mom, Dad is here in the park! He waved to me as if he was saying, 'I am with you.'" I hugged my girl and said, "Yes, he is and always will be here in our hearts forever."

Children are much more aware of death than we realize. It's all around them, really. Their pets die, and dead birds and insects are familiar sights. They see it on television every day and in video games and movies. It's in their fairy tales and in their play. Death is a part of everyday living, and we must let them talk to us about it if we are to help them in the healing process. But first, we must be open, honest, and comfortable with our own feelings.

I now had the solo role of caring for my children, guiding them so they could heal from their loss. I had to be alert for difficult experiences that might affect their healing process. I had to watch to see if they showed any signs of aggression or seemed to be angry with the world or were having any physical symptoms such as headaches or stomach aches. I had to make sure they were still having fun with their friends instead of withdrawing into themselves. On top of that, I had to watch how they were doing in school, not only with their classes but with their behavior.

When I was young, I would look at people in various difficult situations and try to imagine what they were going through. It was difficult to imagine how I would have reacted if my worst nightmare ever happened. At best, I thought and hoped that I would be able to do whatever I needed to do to survive. The truth is, I hoped I never had to find out. Yes, I wanted to die with Flor. I didn't know how to live without his love and support. Living without our Flor was a most difficult burden to carry because I ached not only for myself but for Flor and my children as well. Carrying the burden of loss was horrible. The misery and agony of grief were to take up residency in my soul and in my whole body.

But all of these overwhelming thoughts of the responsibilities that lay ahead were for another time. When I got home from picking up my children and our talk in the park, all of my energy was gone. All I could do was lie down and close my eyes as the pain of my grief took over the whole of my brain. I didn't have the energy to think new thoughts. Miserable grief stole the parts of me I most wanted to share with others — my light, my laughter, my generous heart. I was in a deep pain that burned as if an invisible flame was held against my skin. The joy that used to fill my heart had completely left me. Only the agony and the misery of grief remained.

Relatives and friends came by to try to rescue me in this time of sorrow. My sisters Remy and Luz and my best friend, Lai, were the first to come to hold my hand. My niece Lita and her husband, Allan, and their beautiful children, Rosalie, Lyn, and Rhian, rushed from L.A. to be with me. My friend Lily Villaluna took her very first BART ride to be with me. She also had lost her husband not too long ago. Hedy, a good friend of Flor's, was also there. Sister Carol Bautista from the Cursillo movement came as soon as she heard the news.

Our house was full of people willing to help ease my pain, but nothing could help me. Grief gushed in to overtake my heart and stole my appetite and sleep as well. A terrible pain in my gut never left. It felt like death, and in quiet moments it took the air from my body and dulled my mind. What was once complete now lay in pieces. Where there was once love, there was now complete emptiness. Our love gave us the finest moments and was the greatest gift from Heaven. Flor's love took up residence in my life and my heart, and in his absence that room has remained empty. No one can ever take his place. All my life, I had known only one man who loved me more than life itself. That was Flor. Flor was the world — my world. Without him, I could not enjoy a simple flower or the rising sun.

My thoughts on the night Flor proposed to me tell of the depth of my love for him and will always echo in my heart:

"In your embrace, the world stops still on its axis. There is no time, no wind, no rain. I am truly at peace. Your love is pure, unselfish, undemanding. And free. I felt your body press in, strong and warm. This is the love I waited for, prayed for. I inwardly thanked God and hugged you all the tighter. A love like this is to be cherished for life. Finally, I am home."

April 30, 1984, marked the beginning of the longest, darkest, most fearful night of my soul I have ever lived. I found myself gradually fading, like a dying plant in the desert, thirsty for rain that wasn't there. The song of joy vanished with the sun setting across the horizon, never to shine again.

CHAPTER 26

The World Did Not Stop Revolving

I've read somewhere in a book [that]
when something happens that is unbearable
to you, sometimes time stops, like your inner clock
just stops working; even if the world keeps spinning,
you will stand still for the rest of your life.

— Katja Michael

DEATH CAN DEVASTATE THOSE IT leaves behind, and each person grieves in their own way. It can affect the whole family as well, throwing it off balance, with grieving family members acting in uncharacteristic and sometimes crazy ways. I was one of the lucky ones. Both Flor's family and my own supported me, and they supported each other.

I knew it would take time for Flor's body to arrive from Africa. I stayed home sick. I lay on the couch in our living room and could not get up. Grief had taken over my whole being. My skin lost all of its color — I was chalk-white — and I could not open my eyes. I held my hands over my chest as though I were trying to stop my heart from escaping.

I just lay there in terror, too overwhelmed to move, my forehead sweaty, my stomach aching. As I lay there with my eyes closed, I heard people asking me questions. "Do you think Flor had insurance?" Or "Can you pay the bills now that he is gone?" Or, "Are you going to move?" One woman said, "You should dispose of all of his clothes soon; that will help you heal." Some people said, "It's better not to talk about him so you can forget him soon." I muttered to myself, "Why should I forget him?"

I could not answer these questions; I just wanted to be alone. I could not understand why people even asked questions like that so soon. "How can they be that insensitive?" I said to myself. Some people also suggested that I go to Africa. *But how? I can't even open my eyes. I can't even think,* I thought. Some would ask, "How are you going to take care of your children?" I would have answered, "I don't know," if I had been strong enough to talk. My mother understood how I was feeling, so she told these people that I needed to get to bed upstairs to rest, and in my head, I said, *Thank you, Inay.*

Many remarks meant to be kind were more hurtful than consoling. For example: "How are you doing?" Why would they ask that? Don't they know I just lost the love of my life? How do they think I'm doing? Another said, "I understand how you feel." How could she? She had not lost a husband. And then, "At least he is in a better place now." How could he know that? Even worse: "You have time to find another one." I just hoped they would all shut their mouths.

One that greatly angered me was being called a "beautiful widow." It branded me, and I did not like it. I think people should be taught how to talk to someone going through the grieving process. I am sure they meant well, but it sure hurt. I, for one, did not understand why they talked like that, and I hope I have learned from my experience when it's time for me to open my mouth in such situations.

While I lay in bed, sick with grief, I thought of my children and how people might view them now that Flor was gone. I was now a "single parent," another term like "widow" that labeled me. Most people believe that being a single parent is not good for children. They look at a single parent as being incapable of raising a responsible child. I thought about those nights when Flor and I would talk about how we would care for our children. We both agreed that we would support each other in any decision we made concerning them, an assurance for me that his support would be with me no matter what, and knowing that gave me peace.

Communication in our relationship was really important to us. We talked about everything, so I had some idea of the direction we wanted to take even though he was gone. Maybe that would help me with the raising of the children. And with the budget too. I tried to think ahead because I knew the world would not stop revolving even if I wanted it to. I knew I had to be ready to care for my children. I knew the Earth would continue to spin on its axis, even though my world was standing still. I knew I needed to be strong and ready to fight solo. But for now, I could not even open my eyes.

Thank God my family was there to help me. My Ate Bening decided to stay with me so my kids would be taken care of. My sister Luz stayed for a while to help me with the paperwork related to Flor's death, and Beth, my sister-in-law, helped with all the other paperwork needed to run a household. My brothers-in-law and sisters-in-law who were nearby volunteered to drive my kids wherever they needed to go. Lannie and Scott came to fix our curtains in the master bedroom. My sister Remy and her husband taught me how to drive as soon as I was able. I was grateful for all their help.

CHAPTER 27

Oh, My Children — My Guide, My Hope, My Light

To lose your father is to lose the one
whose guidance and help you seek,
who supports you like a tree supports its branches.

— Yann Martel, Life of Pi

CHILDHOOD SHOULD BE A TIME of simplicity and wonder and safety and love. A time for children to discover their passions, talents, and unique interests. It is the time to lay a solid foundation for a physically healthy life as well as a mentally and emotionally healthy life. It should provide our children the best possible chance to win the you-versus-me battle to put them on the right course to be able to contribute to society. Childhood is the foundation parents need to get right if they want their children to achieve success in the world. Flor and I tried our very best to give our children love and whatever else they needed to provide that solid foundation.

Now that Flor was gone, life was not easy for our children. They tried hard to live without their beloved father, but I knew how they felt every time I saw a cut flower. It didn't have any roots at all, so there was nothing to anchor it in this world, yet it was still expected to flourish, be beautiful, and warm the hearts of others. No one could see my children's pain, their vulnerability, the roots they lacked. They tried their very best to decorate their world with enthusiasm, hugs, laughter, and kindness, but that only masked the anger, fear, and uncertainty underneath.

I vowed to be everything they weren't and to try to give them what they did not have and to give them the security and unconditional love they needed. I begged the Lord above every day to give me the strength to channel His love to my children, the love that had been there but was crushed with the loss of their beloved father. I hoped and prayed every day that my love alone would now be enough for them to have a happy life. Every day, I prayed that one day their hearts would be whole again. I prayed that the God of love would help me find ways to soothe and heal them.

I wanted my children to remember that they were born of stardust and with a divine soul. I wanted them to know they were beings of the same worth as angels, and angels would always watch over them and protect them while they were alone and in pain. I felt then that I could do nothing to help them, and my heart was saying, "I am very sorry. I wish I could do more. I will try my best to come back to love, to the ways of the Divine. Then, and only then, will I have all the hands and feet I could ever need to cuddle and take care of their lonely souls."

My children's grief came to them like ocean waves — small waves at first, but later on, waves so strong that they threatened to sweep my little ones away. Loneliness also came with these waves of grief and replaced what once felt normal to them with tears that were now becoming all too familiar. All we could do as a family to survive was to hold on together with love.

My children's tremendous loss changed them. I've heard it said that there comes a time in life that transforms us, and all we can do is try very hard to learn how to swim with grace and stay in that hostile water. My children tried to be brave and to conquer their fear, slowly accepting it as something to be overcome. They all chose to fight with all their might to survive in the absence of their beloved father.

Melissa, at the young age of eleven, took on so many responsibilities that, in my eyes, belonged only to the courageous. My heart cried for her. She was so young to take on the role of a leader. I wanted her to enjoy her childhood a little more, just as her father and I had planned. But she became the navigator when my sensory fog rolled in. She could tell where "true north" was and felt it too. She tried to become my guide through unmarked territory.

She did her best to help me in taking care of her siblings. She quickly learned all the routes I needed to know to drive them to their different activities, becoming an encouraging and practical source of help to all of us. She was delightful in the ways she helped our family live in harmony with a great understanding of our daily struggles.

She helped me gain a new vision of life as life was then as well as in the future. I saw that she was fearful and unsure of herself at times, but once she learned to put the fear and doubts aside, it was clear that she would survive to enter into a new life after the pain receded. Melissa became my very own light. As I walked through the darkness, I feared no evil as I was guided by the love she provided. She was the one who guided me in the direction of love and away from bitterness.

V.J. was nine years old when his beloved father passed away. My heart went out to him because I knew that as he grew and matured, he would start to grieve all over again. I hoped that he would not go back to the beginning of his grieving process but that he would learn, as I had, that the pain of his father's death was not something that would blow over with time. Rather, it was a part of him and his life moving forward. He wouldn't simply "get over it." I watched V.J. with an eagle eye. He was reminded daily that his dad was not there anymore. Every day was a Code Red day. Every time somebody talked about his dad, his death became more real. And that hurt so much.

V.J. loved playing sports with his dad, especially football and basketball, and played on the St. Agnes basketball and football teams. They practiced every day in the park near our home. One day, he came to me with his football and basketball uniforms in his hands and said, "Mom, I'm not playing these sports anymore." I saw him standing there, his face clouded with sadness and tears in his eyes, but I couldn't say anything at the moment. I glanced upward as tears flooded my eyes. My heart ached for my little boy. "God, please help us," I prayed.

I knew V.J. was hurting and missing his dad and that this was something in his life he had to face on his own. I took a breath and said, "V.J., if that is your decision, I will support you all the way, but I want you to be the one to talk to your coach and explain your decision to him." He nodded and ran to the coach to return his uniforms. When he came back, I hugged him tightly and said, "I am so proud of you, my son." I knew then that my son would have the guts to fight any dragon that would come his way.

Another issue V.J. had to tackle was his schooling. He never liked school. I held his hand every step of the way when he sat down to do his schoolwork. Flor and I were so worried that he would not finish his schooling; he always found excuses not to go. It drove Flor to start smoking. We spent countless hours thinking of what to do as if we held his destiny in our hands.

It was a beautiful day. The sun had found its way from the horizon to the summit of the sky. The birds were soaring high with much zeal, bringing courage to all to hope for a better day. Suddenly, I heard a roaring voice coming from the doorway: "Mom! Mom! You have to be proud of me, Mom!" V.J. rushed toward me with his fourth-grade report card in his hand and a wonderful smile on his face. He was beaming with pride. I looked at the card. "V.J., you made the honor roll! Oh, V.J., I am so proud of you. Keep up the good work!" I said with excitement. I looked up to heaven and smiled because I knew Flor was happy. On this wonderful day, I knew that V.J. was my hope. Hope is seeing beauty in the black night and the power to feel the wonders beyond. Hope is the light that forms a rope that anchors you to the chance of a better future.

Iza, my youngest one, had just turned six when Flor left. It broke my heart that she probably would not remember how her father adored her. When she was born, he even said, "This baby can sing. I will give her my song." Like her dad, Iza did love to sing. She was a cheerful and playful child, and her black hair glistened when the sun shone on it.

I wanted to include my children in the funeral service by having them share their thoughts about their dad so they could finally say goodbye. I thought that remembering their dad in such a way would help in the process of healing. Each of my children had a different way of grieving, and Iza could not talk about her dad. What Iza did was write down her thoughts and feelings. I was so glad she found a way to express her fear and pain through writing.

It was a day when the burning midday sun shone relentlessly on the sidewalk, and the street seemed to sizzle in the heat. Tall, sunlit buildings pierced the hot blue sky. Iza came to me with a tiny, colorful book in her hand. "Mom, I wrote this book. Isn't it colorful?" she said excitedly.

I took a look at this red, green, and brown book so carefully crafted by my little girl. "Oh, wow! I love this," I said.

"You can read it, Mom," she said excitedly.

I took a seat on the sofa close to the window to relax and read the book. It was about a little girl whose dad went to work one day and did not come home. The little girl wrote to Santa to bring her dad back on Christmas Day. It was a book of wishes that came from Iza's heart. My eyes flooded with tears as I read this book because I could feel through her writing her longing to see her dad. I was grateful that she found a way to express her longing as it would help her heal. Iza continued to write in her journal to ease her pain. She continued to be playful in spite of everything. She became my light on this journey of pain and tribulation. Author Og Mandino wrote: "I will love the light, for it shows me the way, yet I will endure the darkness because it shows me the stars."

Melissa, V.J., Iza — they became my guides, my hope, and my light as I navigated this unknown territory, a painful journey of a thousand miles that must be taken only one step at a time. Yes, one step at a time, and I believe the best view comes after the hardest climb.

To help my children on their journey, I searched for inspiration and guidance. I found this advice by Christian Larson in his book *Your Forces and How to Use Them*:

Promise Yourself
To be so strong that nothing
can disturb your peace of mind.

To talk health, happiness, and prosperity
to every person you meet.

To make all your friends feel that there is something good in them.
To look at the sunny side of everything
and make your optimism come true.

To think only of the best, to work only for the best,
and expect only the best.
To be just as enthusiastic about the success of others
as you are about your own.

To forget the mistakes of the past
and press on to the greater achievements of the future.
To wear a cheerful countenance at all times
and give every living creature you meet a smile.

To give so much time to the improvement of yourself
that you have no time to criticize others.
To be too large for worry, too noble for anger, too strong for fear,
and too happy to permit the presence of trouble.

I continued to watch all of my children with love and compassion to make sure they didn't fall into a deep depression. I watched to see if they were sleeping too much, if their eating habits had changed, if they were keeping up their grades, or if they were losing interest in their friends and activities. I wanted to know when they were sad, angry, or depressed. I believed I could better help them to survive this ordeal if I could be aware early on of any problems that might arise.

I am so grateful for my children and for the journey we have been on, remembering that love prevails if everything else fails.

CHAPTER 28

Life Must Go On

Why does my heart go on beating? . . .
Why does the sun go on shining?
Why does the sea rush to shore? . . .
Don't they know it's the end of the world?
It ended when you said, "Goodbye."

— *"The End of the World," lyrics by Sylvia Dee,*
as sung by Skeeter Davis

UNDER A SHADE SO GENTLE between clouds and baby-blue sky, I observed each bird on its wing. It was one of those Eastertide days with a soul kiss of coldness that heightened the warm rays of the sun. I paused to admire the flowers and sense their fragrance to be in the moment with their beauty. The flowers and everything beyond them should have brought happiness. But today, I did not feel anything. Instead, I questioned their existence. Why did the Earth keep on spinning? Why did the sun go on shining? Why did the birds go on singing? Didn't they know that I lost my beloved? I wanted everything in the world to stop. "There is no use for them to go on anymore. They could all be gone for all I care," I said to myself.

Once, I was a woman who had felt the Divine within the love I gave to my ideas and the artistic ways I expressed my soul. I used to fold my arms around the soul of the world and all who loved me and those who needed love. But all that changed in the blink of an eye. Now I could not even think. My heart was shattered into a million pieces. Every day was a battle. The overwhelming sadness and emptiness were too much to bear. I struggled just to get out of bed. Every day, a part of me wanted to cry out, and another part wanted to hit something with the anger that was raging inside me. At times, losing my beloved was like having a hole drilled into my heart, the pain flaring up like a fire. At other times, it felt like my heart had been replaced with ice and electricity had been wired straight into my spine. My heart felt like it had been ripped apart — all the time. It was too painful.

When God took my beloved, I felt so alone and abandoned. Yes, abandoned. Because that's what people on the outside saw, people who didn't know my story, and then they made harsh judgments as to why I was so alone. Let me open my heart and soul so that you can understand what being abandoned meant to me.

At first, there was the screaming of my spirit, the begging on my bended knee for the soul-shattering, invisible hemorrhaging to stop. And the promise to do anything not to suffer. Then there was the fracturing of my brain, the plummeting of my emotions that pushed and pulled, followed by the deterioration of my self-respect and self-control. It hurt. It was a pain that I had not experienced before. It hurt every day, every moment, until my brain stopped yearning for love and began to reject its cure — because I had experienced true love from my beloved very deeply, and it hurt knowing he was not coming back. I will always remember how it felt to be so deserted.

This transformation was so very painful and difficult for my sensitive heart because I tried to fight it. I clung to love, to the smallest whisper of a chance for love. And our love was the kind that would have weathered any storm to remain true. For that kind of love, I would rather die than be abandoned. So, please, when you find a soft-hearted person alone, be kind and wrap them in your loving arms and understand that they are going through so much pain and agony that would even be too much for the lowest of creatures.

My friends from work were worried about me. Bette, my boss, a beautiful woman with a very understanding heart and a great smile, visited me one day to talk to me about coming back to work. "Thelma, I want you to come back to work on the Monday after Flor's funeral on Saturday," she said. "The way I see you, you can't even get up from bed. I don't want you to stay this way. Remember, you are the sole provider now. That job entails a lot of decision-making. You have to be alert and alive to do the job. Staying in bed and not using your brain is not ideal at this time."

I looked at her and sighed. "I don't know, Bette," I answered. "I can't even think straight."

"I understand," she answered calmly, "but I want you to realize that you need to get up and start living again, not only for yourself but for your children, too."

"Okay, Bette," I said softly, trying to call on every ounce of strength that I had. "I will try."

"Don't worry about the work. Your friends volunteered to help you until you are ready. They are all very supportive of you. You must have been a very good person," she said jokingly.

"I guess so," I said, trying to force a little smile.

The day of Flor's funeral came. My doctor had given me something to calm me down so I could be supportive of my children, to show them we could make it without their beloved father. All of my sisters and brothers, as well as all my brothers-in-law and sisters-in-law, were there to support me. I tried my best to get up and walk calmly, but my body wouldn't let me. I felt so weak. I felt so much pain in my heart and in every part of my body. I was hurting — a hurt that I had never felt before. I could not explain this pain. Terror held me captive. I felt nauseated and dizzy. I could not hold myself up. Sweat beaded my forehead, and my eyes flooded with tears. I tried to hold my head up, but it wouldn't let me. I felt so weak and unable to breathe. Fear engulfed my whole being.

I stood outside the room in the funeral parlor where we were gathered and listened to Tatay, Flor's dad, crying as if his brains were being shredded. Emotional pain flowed out of his every pore. His cry was so raw that even the eyes of the strangers around him were wet with tears. His children, I am sure, grabbed hold of him so that his violent shaking would not cause him to fall. I could imagine the tears coming from his eyes as I heard him say, "Why, Lord, why him? Why not me? I would trade places with him. I am old. His family needs him." He cried in anguish. We expect to bury our parents, not our children. My niece Lita, a nurse, talked to him, but it did no good. The whole world seemed to vanish for him; now there was only pain, enough to break him.

My mom and Nanay (Flor's mom) cried as if the ferocity of it might bring him back to life. People around them tried to appease them, but their hysteria was uncontrollable. Their wailing carried through the damp air outside.

In the cemetery, my grief surged with every expelled breath, always reaching a higher peak, never sufficiently soothed by my prolonged intake of the damp spring air. Tears began to spill from my helpless eyes onto the ground. My gaze swept from bloom to bloom. At that moment, the sure knowledge that life would go on without my beloved undid me completely. All the pretense of quiet coping was lost, and I sank to the bench, hunched over and with a sense of loss so powerful that my muscles would not respond to my commands. I bit my lips to keep from crying. I felt a searing pain in my heart. I was in a state of misery, and I could not see the end. There was an aura of gray around me, a fog that found a permanent place in my heart. My life and the lives of our children would never be the same. I cast my eyes to the Lord. I needed His love more than ever. "Dear God, take care of my beloved husband." At that moment, all hope vanished; the only thing left for me was sadness and pain. It was painful even to pray. All beauty and grandeur on the horizon vanished, never to be seen again.

I had promised Bette that I planned to go to work on the Monday following the funeral. The carpool van was going to pick me up, and I waited in front of my house, looking like a zombie. Suddenly, I realized this was my life now. Flor was not there with me. He used to be with me every day while I waited for this van. The thought of him not being there with me made me scared, so scared, like every breath of wind was as loud as a blood-curdling scream.

This was the most terrifying day of my life. I felt so alone. "Please help me, honey. I need you," I whispered. I tried to steady my breath to calm the panic. My heart was pounding in my ears. I tried to scream, but I couldn't. I wanted to go back inside the house, but my feet wouldn't let me. Sweat streamed down my body as I stood still. "I don't think I can go anywhere today," I said to myself. My throbbing heart was loud and irregular, but I barely heard it because my mind was clouded with fear.

"I cannot live life without Flor," I whispered to myself. "I cannot do this. I'd better go back inside the house." I tried again to walk back in, but just then the van arrived. My sister-in-law Beth, the wife of my youngest brother, Sonny, stepped out of the van to help me. "Ate," she said softly. "I will take you to the van. You can do this."

Beth lived a couple of blocks from my house, worked in San Francisco, and van-pooled with us every day. She was one of my great supporters. She was a beautiful, petite woman with a very friendly smile. She had been there for me ever since the news of Flor's death. She tried to help me with everything she could. She made sure all the papers that needed to be taken care of were safe and organized. I felt a little better as she held my hand and walked with me to the van. I was able to go to work that day but was still in a state of sorrow and pain, still very much heartbroken, lost, and bereaved. I knew my own helplessness. I could not function and be in deep despair.

Life seemed so unfair. All I held in my hands now was a bucketful of sorrow. That's the thing, a stunning thing: Some of us carry these tragic loads that seem too heavy to lift even once, yet we must carry them alone and forevermore. The sad anger is always there. Anger at God for making my life like this. Anger because He took Flor back so soon.

"What did I do wrong?" I asked. "I tried so hard to be a good daughter, a good wife, a good mother. What does God want me to be? Why is this pain not only for me but for my children — for the whole family? What about my children? Did God forget that *we* have children?"

People told me that God would help people like me who were in desperate need of help, but what I was fully aware of then was that God had not yet done His work. Unless he considered the marvel that I was here at work, moving like a zombie spirit, his handiwork. Trying every day to overcome this heartbreaking experience was awful and seemed to take forever. I felt like the world was caving in on me. I could not breathe.

True to their word, my coworkers helped me until I was able to function. I was amid fields of sorrow and pain. Coming to know the true face of friendship was one of the many blessings of grief.

CHAPTER 29

The Greatest Fear

Be afraid of nothing. You have within you all wisdom,
all power, all strength, all understanding.

— *Eileen Caddy*

MY BELOVED HUSBAND, FLOR, had given me the most incredible blessing heaven could give — real love. In his love, there was beauty. Whatever I did was right and in the right order. His love was always fresh, new, alive, as if there were no yesterdays and no tomorrows. There was no more striving, there were no more needs to chase after, because in him there was that real love. Yes, the greatest blessing of all.

Losing him so fast left me in a state of shock and terror. Fear tormented me every time I thought about him. My greatest fear was not being able to be myself again. I wanted to be myself when he was alive — confident, self-assured, always in good spirits, very positive in my ideas and strong in mind, body, and spirit. He always admired those characteristics in me. He was so proud of me. But now, I am a mess. I could not function or think right. Every day, I fought a rising panic. I trembled inside as terror continued to stab my heart.

This greatest fear paralyzed and tormented me every day. There were days when my frustration built to such a point that I thought I might explode. I wanted to shout, throw a tantrum, break something, or beat my hands on the ground like an angry child. I wanted to speak out, but I didn't want to say something I didn't really mean and be hurtful. Every day, I felt the fear in my chest waiting to take over. It sat there like an angry bull, propelling me into the anxiety I just didn't need.

My sadness, my fear, my love — they were raptors flying around in my head. I felt so alone, isolated. There were days and days of fear and sadness visiting me with their melancholy melody, and I stood there listening until I broke into pieces again and again.

Yes, I wanted these feelings erased completely from my mind, not for me but for my children. Our children were made from love. I wanted to get up and be strong for my children's sake. They were so young and hurting, but my body and my mind wouldn't let me. I was still mourning, and it was not good. It was only the start of my longest and darkest journey. Tears came, hot and endless, every day. I believed that life was the most sacred of all gifts heaven could bestow upon me and all of creation, but only in the presence of love. Without Flor, love was completely gone.

Most nights, I could not sleep. I would fall asleep only after being awake for a very long time. The sleep deprivation became painful. My brain was in so much pain, but I felt that it must keep working to keep me safe. I needed a reboot, a time away from stress. My body and my brain needed to feel safe to solve all of the problems I needed to solve in order to survive, to live, not for myself but for my children.

I knew the roles of being a mother and a father were God-given and natural. Both love. Both protect. Yet their tasks are split because of the vulnerability that motherhood brings. I realized why, in times of war, the man traditionally goes into battle first. If the father fails to return, then the mother steps up. Mama Bear comes out with claws and teeth and all her strength because she has to stand between her children and whatever is coming over the hill. I knew I had a mission to fulfill. How to do it was the question.

My life at that time had been akin to sprinting through the fog — unable to sleep at night but getting up early in the morning to work. Moving like a zombie, painfully slow, mindless, and unguided.

One day, I slowly took my seat at the back of the van and closed my eyes. Suddenly, Flor, my beloved, hopped into the van and came to where I was sitting. "Honey," he said to me, "you have not been sleeping for a long time. I pray that you don't get sick. I know you are very sad because God took me."

He continued to talk to me. "Honey, you know I tried my best to refuse His calling because I thought of you and the kids. Please understand that He is God, and I could not refuse Him."

I looked up to see his face. It was peaceful, and there was an aura of hope and tranquility that surrounded him.

"Come with me, my darling. I want you to see where I am. It might pacify your mind knowing where I am."

He held my hand gently. I could feel his love under my skin and throughout my being. It was the best feeling I had felt since he had left. I felt so complete. *Oh, I wish I could keep this feeling forever,* I thought. I felt weightless as he held my hand.

"Honey," he said, "there is your itay. He is so happy here."

I saw my father. He looked so young and healthy. He smiled and waved his hand. I felt his love in my heart. *I am at peace. This must be heaven,* I thought.

"Honey, please don't be afraid that you will be alone because I already asked the Lord to give me a dispensation to stay with you for a while. I told him that you cannot do it alone, and He agreed. Our children are very small, so I will be with you always. Don't worry, and trust that all will be well in God's time," he said gently.

I looked around while he held my hand. *So, this is Heaven,* I thought. In this place, I saw snow come, white and glistening, to erase the troubles beneath it, directing me toward a new and positive way. The coldness only quickened my resolve to find love again. Perhaps, while Flor was holding my hand so gently, in this swirling, perfect whiteness that gave perfect, crystalline kisses, the coolness in the air might rejuvenate my soul, elevate my spirit, and give me a new reason to step forward with confidence, to stand strong with his love in my heart. It may have been winter, but there was beauty in it, clarity, that kind of clear thinking that let me notice small details, like how the trees, though bare, had the promise of spring within them, as if the

Creator Himself lay dormant in the branches, ready to burst forth and greet the world with His many hues of green. As the sun crept over the horizon, I felt more optimistic than ever before. There was still a flame in my soul, burning with love, always ready to start a new blaze. I closed my eyes and felt the positive ions flow, recharging my neurons until they rekindled and sparked. I heard Flor talking again, so gentle, so full of love and affection. I felt it in my heart.

"Honey, when you learn to resonate your mind with your soul, you will live through a love that's so honest it's raw. In the beginning, you will be as a child in the wintry wind, pulling your clothes close around you, seeking shelter. But hold on tight to our beautiful love and the memories we built together because in time you will be as a child in the most beautiful of gardens, enchanted by the blooms, laughing with a joy that leaps and twirls. So, honey, be brave and grow strong by having faith and love in your own heart as your guide. And, my love, should you ever need a light to show you the way, I will be there always, helping you to light your own path.

"Honey, together we will flood your being with love. It will run in your veins, and it will shine bright. Do not worry, honey. Soon, you will have the confidence of a phoenix, of one who has suffered and been burned by flames of hot pain, one who rises from their own ashes reborn and commanded to sing. This is the confidence, hard-won yet deep, anchored in the true self that is always safe in our core. It is that which grows within, purging that which is born of fear, clearing the way for love to grow and to make up every aspect of who you are.

"I believe with all my heart that you can do this because I will be with you all the way as we are truly one. Let us reach out with love because love heals, love makes us whole. Love elevates us to better and more noble thoughts. Honey, remember that I love you so much. Be strong with that love. Hold on tight. Remember, the glass is still half-full, and I know we can make it if we try."

Suddenly, I heard the van driver say, "Thelma, wake up. This is your stop."

I opened my eyes and felt refreshed, as if I had been guided to a fresh start. I felt blessed. I regretted that I had to wake up but then remembered what Flor had said: "I promise to be with you on your journey, honey. I will be with you always." That thought gave me peace, and I was ready to face the day and ready for a fresh start.

A fresh start was the weirdest thing for me, as if everything that had happened up to this point was a prequel in the series of books that was my life. It felt as if one book closed and a new one opened, one word after another appearing slowly on the page with a calmness the first volumes never possessed.

It came naturally, like music, like drops of rain upon a swath of leaves, chaotic and rhythmic at once. And as the words formed, in deepest blue dancing over a white page, they were like dance steps, my motion deliberate and intuitive yet guided by the ever-present music. This was the way of everything, the chaos, the synchrony, the guidance, and all with a sprinkle of destiny. I knew that, with Flor's love and guidance, I could try my best, be where I was supposed to be, always be a part of the best story I was able to write. I could be a child in this universe, woven into the fabric of creation. And there was serenity in that. It was a blessing to allow light to shine in me, to step forward, face the fear with confidence and allow every scar to heal until I was strong from my core all the way to my skin.

I found wisdom in keeping my blessings close, in the heartland of my mind. I saw how the universe conspired to help those who struggled to become the best version of themselves in order to help others. I realized now that I was not alone on my journey. I could look at fear and say, "You can never keep me captive now that I know that my beloved is with me now and forever." With love in my heart and a mission to accomplish, I held on to my faith, because in faith I was free. I felt the divinity of my God-given talent and saw how I could do good things for other people, especially my children. Every chain had broken, and I was free.

I started to do things to gain a better understanding of my fear because I knew that emotional growth was much akin to physical fitness. I wanted to be more empathetic and kind, and I knew that, just as when strengthening the body's muscles, the more I did the right things, even as they became more challenging, the easier it would get. The idea of "no pain, no gain" also applied because I had to be willing to look at myself with a "no excuses" attitude and be willing to make changes as needed. I was not perfect yet.

My difficult emotions were like a river flowing by me. I sat on the grass and onward they went. In a few days, the water would be calm again, and so would I. I learned that there was nothing to be done about this. I could just stay calm, do healthy things, and everything would be okay again. Love truly has a healing power that lights up the mind and generates a kind of vision that could be called an emotional sunrise.

Every day, I was forever grateful that God had given me Flor as Flor's love was so strong and warm that I was slowly becoming a version of myself that I had given up as lost. Our love was a sort of magic, and I was grateful for that magic in my soul. His love had given me hope when there was no light — indeed, when there was nothing beyond the boundaries of my skin. The hope he gave me was like a word written in heaven's vibration that spoke right to my healing soul. There was something about the idea of hope, so full of meaning. I tried to cling to it even though deep in my brain, deep in my heart, it was beyond my understanding. Then something happened. Hope healed. Our love made a cocoon and broke it open when I was ready to fly.

I became a girl on a walk, starting to get a feel again for who I was at my core. The days became calmer now that I had mastered the art of having a clear mind. I was now blessed with the serenity of feeling my intelligence rather than tiring myself out with unresolved thoughts. I could see more clearly through my essence, not through my eyes, a sort of thinking without words. What came to me were pure thoughts, a sort of poetry I never realized I was capable of. I became the girl who felt more in charge, more in command of my own body, mind, and spirit. I became the girl walking to a destiny that lay squarely in my own hands. I became the girl that Flor had fallen in love with and more, a girl who was the captain of her own life and future. It was a beautiful sight.

I will always face fear with courage, understand it, and then let it go. I had allowed this fear to wake me up. I let it show me the way to my true self, to the brave soul whose love shines like a star. Because without fear, love is brighter, stronger, and deeper. Once I found myself, I became my own master, fully healed, and now my fear would be my strength.

CHAPTER 30

Fireballs of Grief

Grief has a way of removing you from the world,
and it takes a real strength to reconnect and weave
yourself anew into the fabric of living, to give yourself
a chance of future happiness.

— *Angela Abraham*

IT WAS A BIG, big challenge for me to even think about navigating through my grief in the midst of such immense changes. Grief doesn't magically end at a certain point in time. When my beloved died, I faced the grief of losing him again and again. Feelings of grief returned unexpectedly throughout the years. I called these unexpected visits "fireballs of grief." They always brought back the pain of my loss.

These fireballs were reminders that my loved one's life was important to me and that I'd had with him the love affair of my lifetime. Like today. I woke up in the morning, and the sun was brighter than on other recent days. I could hear the birds chirping and enjoying the cool breeze on this December morning. The dewdrops were falling from the leaves of my plants out in the garden. What a beautiful morning it was. Milky clouds came for a visit and traveled around the sky above as if the creative, golden sun got up like a five-year-old child and started to paint over the dark black night until it was a bright, beautiful day.

"It is going to be a perfect day," I said to myself as I rushed to my walk-in closet. I was surprised to find the most beautiful yellow flowers there. Yellow, my favorite color. My heart raced a thousand miles an hour.

Who put these flowers here? I wondered, looking at the card: "Happy Anniversary, Mom!"

"Wow!" I said to myself. "They remembered!"

The scent of the flowers was like the sting of Cupid's arrows, which come at random times and in plain sight, always on target. The sweet aroma, this fragrance, woke up those beautiful memories of love kept in my soul. Today, I shed tears but happy tears, because the love of my husband was being channeled through my children, reminding me that our love is still alive and will be with us forever. A true-life story of love and loss.

These fireballs have provided shelter on many lonely nights during the grieving process. They are what brought me to where I am today, a constant hint that true love really exists. They are messages that love wins when everything else fails. These are the reassuring pats on the back that all will be well in time.

But these fireballs are not always kind. A fireball of grief can also ignite in me feelings of anger and anxiety, set me to crying, make me lose my motivation for anything, and make me feel lonely. A fireball of grief can happen anytime and anywhere. Although some may be obvious and predictable, others hit me unexpectedly, like a giant wave, and have often knocked me down. Like the day Iza sang at my niece's wedding. She sang so beautifully, like a member of a choir of angels. The harsh fireball came rushing to my heart as I thought about Flor's desire for Iza to develop her singing voice. After all, he had given her his song. When I heard her sing, I ached for my beloved. He had missed out on this beautiful occasion. He had missed out on seeing his dream come true. And that pained me for days. Sometimes on this journey, I hurt not only for myself but also for Flor and the children. Sometimes, the pain came as a triple threat. Fireballs come and go, but as always, I cling to love that rises when all else fails.

Many times, fireballs of grief that came out of the blue would remind me of my loss and cause me to mourn all over again, leaving me sad, depressed, or anxious. I needed to learn how to minimize these effects and how to be ready for these unpredictable episodes. I bought a journal to record what I could to help keep me from returning to a state of deep melancholy. I found it sometimes helpful to plan a distraction, like going out with friends or doing anything interesting to distract myself. I also learned to reframe the way I talked to myself and about myself, mitigating the effects of those fireballs with positive thinking. Eventually, though, I found out that it was better to face the fireballs and allow myself to feel the pain in acknowledgment that there was no timeline in my grieving process. That thought often gave me peace.

Fireballs were triggered not only by events, special dates, flowers, pictures, and memories, but also the presence of people. Men who wanted to be more than friends with me could trigger a fireball. They awakened the memory of Flor and our love affair, and the memories of that love brought anxiety and sadness to my being. My heart had died with Flor, and the suitors trying to revive my dying heart brought me only more and more heartache. They never understood the kind of love Flor and I had. They never understood why I wanted them to go away. I did not want them because they became the cause of my fear of the unknown, the biggest fireball ever, and I definitely did not want to have any part of that. I was told: "You have to start dating now. Your kids will leave you eventually, so you'd better find somebody; otherwise, you will be alone when your kids leave you." This brought me anxiety and fear. Those types of remarks, I know, were innocent, but they hurt me terribly. I wished the people who made them would just keep their opinions to themselves. Those remarks became one of the many fireballs that brought back the grief, grief that not only affected my life but the lives of my beautiful children as well.

The biggest and the most destructive fireball is being a widow, a constant reminder that I had someone I loved with all my heart and soul but lost him. Being a widow, I didn't always know what to do, such as in parenting my children. There was no manual for widows to help me navigate my new status. There were so many unknowns in this brand-new role that I was forced into after Flor's death. I could see only what my life had been in the past and what it was in the present, but never what my life might become in the future. In the process of grieving, I tried to do everything on my own but, in doing so, I almost lost our house and the lives of my children because I didn't ask for help even though I knew I was really exhausted.

What happened that time was that I volunteered to make the adobo for a fundraiser for V.J.'s school, De La Salle High School. I fell asleep while waiting for the adobo to cook. When I woke up, the house was full of smoke. I could barely breathe. I heard V.J. running outside, carrying his sister to safety. Luckily, I was able to turn off the stove in time to prevent the fire. That night, I learned two things. One is that I can't do everything by myself. The other is that V.J. truly loves his sister. That feels good.

I spent so many sleepless nights on this journey of widowhood. Sleepless nights became an invitation to think deeply about my life and the lives of my children. I spent those hours asking myself what wasn't working and how to make our lives better. I realized that a sleepless night was a chance to meditate, to feel the energy of the positive world asking to come in and let my dreams become my nighttime reality. In the quiet of a sleepless night, I could feel and see the starlight that illuminated the velvety sky. The chamber of worries opened to show me a vision of a new and better world for me and my children. In the stillness of the night, I found ways to put my worries in proper perspective, to adapt, to overcome.

During that time that I call "the darkest night of my soul," I spent so many sleepless nights thinking of my children and their future, my relationship to other people, my relationship with my in-laws, my career, my life, and even my budget. I had so many things that needed attention.

My children — their physical, mental, spiritual, and intellectual states — became my priority. They became my reason for living, the very essence of my life. Through them, I learned the lessons of being a single parent. They taught me to trust and fight with all my might to protect what was truly theirs. Unfortunately, it's not easy for a single mother to do all of these things. Some Filipino parents do not believe that single parents can be good parents on their own. My greatest hurdle in being a single parent, even more than the budgeting, was the presence of other people who took me down a notch because I was alone caring for my children. I remember when Melissa was in high school, she came home crying, saying "My friend's father won't let my friend go with me to the school dance because he said I am always with some boys."

"Boys?" I asked surprisingly. "Who are they?"

"Uncle Jaime and my cousin Mark," she said through her tears.

"Did you tell him that those boys are your uncle and your cousin?" I asked.

"I can't, Mom. He won't listen to me. He said, 'Maybe your mom let you be with those boys because she doesn't know what she is doing, but you cannot take my daughter with you.'

"So I left crying. He would not listen to me."

At that moment, a scream came from deep within me that forced its way to the surface. I hurriedly found my car keys and drove to the man's house. When I knocked on his door, all I felt was anger, as if my soul had unleashed a demon. I felt like a lioness fighting for her cub the best way she could. I looked at this big, tall man and said firmly, "My daughter came home crying because you accused her of hanging out with the boys. Did you know those boys are her uncle and cousin?"

My goal was to protect my daughter as well as my reputation. My voice was loud, even thunderous. A look of great bitterness swept across my face, and I became a different person. All I felt was anger. This guy was so surprised that all he could say was, "I am sorry for not giving her a chance to explain."

I replied in a firm but angry tone: "Don't you ever make any accusation against any of my children ever again. If you have any questions, you can call me because I am the only one who takes care of them — no one else."

From then on, no one questioned my child-rearing abilities. Rumors travel faster than lightning. The word got out: "She fights like a lioness." I realized then that there is no greater warrior than a mother protecting her child.

My children taught me to be strong and stand my ground to protect them. I learned new lessons in caring for their emotions as well as their physical well-being. I tried to teach them the value of education. It would be their golden ticket in life, a chance to better themselves, to learn and grow, to believe in and strive for. They all helped me to survive somehow, and I loved them so much. I wanted to give them the best of everything.

The education of my children became an absolute priority, although the money issue presented a challenge. I tried very hard to budget so I could save for college, but this was not easy for a single mother to do. It was quite challenging and demanded a great deal of courage. The budget was tight. I would have loved to have treated them to eating out sometimes, but I couldn't because I was focused on saving for their college education. Those days were hard for me. I wanted to give them everything, but I couldn't. Their lunch for school was not like the other students' lunches. Sometimes it was only hard-boiled eggs, not like the others, who had sandwiches, pizza, or other tasty snacks. Luckily for us, my mother was a great cook, so we always had good-tasting food, however humble, at every meal. The fear of my kids not finishing college was always on my mind, but I came to let God handle their future because I couldn't do it.

Sometimes it scares me to hope for higher education for my children. *What if I fail to save enough money for their education? What will happen? Will they have to put their goals on hold? What should I do? If they didn't finish their education, what would happen then?*

While questioning my capabilities, I remembered a quote by Jean Shinoda Bolen: "Before you can do something that you've never done, you have to be able to imagine it is possible." With that thought in my mind, I took on the challenge of imagining it was possible to truly help my children.

When my children and I started to take small steps toward our goals and dreams, we entered a new place. We were on a new road and began to see possibilities and solutions that did not seem to be available before. A new world seemed to open for us. As the great Henry David Thoreau said: "If one advances confidently in the direction of his dream, and endeavors to live the life which he has imagined, he will meet with a success unexpected in common hours."

Our family started to show some signs of healing. We became braver, like soldiers fighting our own battles. One beautiful morning told us in various ways that every day of our life was a beginning, and we embraced each day one at a time and saw the beauty of the treasures that unfolded before us.

V.J. approached me and said excitedly, "Mom, I am going to play football at De La Salle."

I looked at him with a smile and said, "Really, V.J.? I heard they are undefeated."

"Yes, Mom, they are," he answered.

I was elated. This was the first time V.J. would be playing any sport since he surrendered his uniforms when he was nine, right after his father died. V.J. was fifteen at the time. He was not as tall as the other players, but I did hope that he would get a chance to play for this number-one team. I thought it would be good for him as I figured he was starting to heal a little bit.

"Okay, V.J., do your best and hope for the best. I will be there for you always," I said as I gave him a big hug.

He was picked to be a running back. I got worried when I saw those big boys on the field. I went to the coach to ask why they picked this little boy to be a running back. The coach answered me with confidence: "Ma'am, he is fast, and he is not a liability." I felt better then, but I vowed to be at every game just in case he got hurt. I rearranged my work schedule so I could make it to his games. That meant starting work at five a.m. to make it to games at two o'clock. I was so blessed to be able to do that. God is good.

Iza, too, was showing some signs of improvement. She became a cheerleader and was picked as the football team queen. She seemed to be talking more now, and best of all, she began to ask questions about her dad, which was an improvement. I heard her singing more and more. These happy tunes melted my heart with joy.

Melissa, who believed that education could open one's eyes and expand the mind more than anything else, was finally at the University of San Francisco. She was studying nursing, her lifelong dream. I was so proud.

And so I began my role as the mother of a young adult, a new role that I had to explore. My life had become a life of never-ending explorations, sometimes exhausting but always worthwhile. I realized that I needed to learn to communicate well with Melissa. I tried to fit our conversations into her schedule, but with her being in college, it was hard. I tried to highlight our common interests. I tried my best not to sound like I was giving a sermon or a lecture. Oftentimes, I prayed to the Lord to show me how to communicate with her effectively without being overprotective. These were the days I wanted Flor by my side because I did not like to sound like I was overprotective. Melissa, thank the Lord, had a good head on her shoulders and knew that I loved her very much.

From my experience in dealing with an adult child, I learned that if I listened to the whisper of my soul and took a very small step forward, a new solution would come. I didn't always do that without fear. I learned to have courage. Sometimes, I had to be willing to move into new and unknown territory and look my fears in the face. That way, my spirit challenged me to grow. I began more and more to trust in my prayers. I finally learned to "pray and let God worry."

CHAPTER 31

The Powerful Effects of Faith

I am still far from being what I want to be,
but with God's help I shall succeed.

— *Vincent van Gogh*

LIFE AFTER FLOR CAME as a wind rolling over bouncing waves, caressing me with a bitterness that brought wakefulness and an awareness of the moment at which I had arrived. Life for me has not opened like a present with pretty wrappings and a promise of comfort. It's been a road of exploration and adventures, with a high degree of misty haze and bitterness. It takes a strong heart and valiant feet to walk this road with my eyes wide open to its twists and turns. I learned to plant my life in love. Then, and only then, was I able to find a cool breeze and raindrops to be refreshing.

My life journey has been a long and crooked road, including countless long days of being so alone. I thought I would feel the sharp blade in my back forever, the long sword slicing into my sensitive flesh. There were days my brain felt fried, so bleary, and the pain, that emotional pain, was all so agonizing. I found myself simply excited when people told me I would come out of this stronger, and I guess that was true, I did. But I came out better than that. I came out wise too. I still have my loving heart. I am happy to say I still have my aspirations, my dreams, and my courage.

My leap of faith did not come easily as I had been used to walking through the fog. But somehow, I found faith enough to allow our Father in Heaven to become exceedingly genuine to me, as authentic as the great Mother herself, as authentic as the evergreens, the ocean, the heavens. I had only to open my eyes, my mind, and my heart to the power of God's love, and there He was, healing the wounds and the pain I thought would never heal. I was finally able to put my trust in our Father, my Maker. I found the reality that our Creator is love, truth, blessings, peace, forgiveness, and joy. I chose to lay down my fears and anxieties at His feet so that He could help me to resolve them and remain His child in mind, heart, and soul.

I could not have done this without the help of my fellow Cursillistas — Sister Evelyn Layola, Sister Sally Reyes, Sister Carol Bautista, Sister Amy Tano, Sister Linda Maerina, Sister Cynthia Bautista, Sister Bea Delgadillo, and Sister Norma — or without my friends in OMI missionary (Oblates of Mary Immaculate), who have the mission to bring good news of Christ to the poor — Sister Bebs Delos Santos, Rose Jardin, Nemia Nicer, Eugene Vallarta, Lily Villaluna, Sister Violy, Father Arong, Brother Mar Tano, and so many more sisters and friends who offered prayers and support. I could not have gone through my healing without the help of these beautiful people, and I am so grateful.

Although the pain comes and goes, the memories of love still linger. I find it refreshing to be able to think of Flor with so much love now and with less pain. I still worry about whether I have raised our children well, but I have learned to forgive myself if, in the process of raising them, I made mistakes, because I tried my very best. And so, many lessons were learned. Most of all, I have gained a deeper understanding of what it is to be a mother through the agony and misery of grief. I could see the pain in my children's eyes as they tried their very best to hold back their tears to protect my broken heart.

Now I understand that people do not know what to say to people in need. I learned that real empathy, instead of insisting that everything will be okay, is sometimes acknowledging that it will not be. I have learned to ask for help. Those closest to me, such as my sister Luz, my Ate Bening, my sister Remy, my sister-in-law Beth, and my brother Sonny, took over when I couldn't move or think. They planned, they arranged, they even told me to eat or sit. They are still doing so much to help me. I have learned about the fireballs of grief that come and go which will be in my life forever, except that now I know how to manage them.

I have learned that grief affects not only my life but the lives of the people around me. My very best friend in elementary school said on one of her visits as an adult: "Thel, this will be my last visit to you because my heart breaks every time I see you cry."

I looked at her and said, "That's okay. Just pray for me." I realize that those connections have changed. I know that people wanted to help, but they didn't know how. I needed to find a way to let people in. I had to let them know they could ask questions and that I would answer them honestly.

In the process of healing, I finally let go and let God. I learned that to trust in God is to truly believe that there is a friendly, abundant, loving energy that supports me and wants the best for me and my children. Letting my fears, concerns, wishes, and prayers go to God means that I trust Him and will work with Him. In that, I find peace.

One of the effects of my faith manifested in my daughter Melissa's graduating from college. It was a great day, a perfect day. She was finally becoming a nurse. I was so proud of her accomplishment. Melissa will face new challenges, but I have faith that God's blessings will go with her, and I trust that life will be good for her.

I continued to hold on to my faith and became a leader in the Cursillo movement in April 1995, eleven years after Flor's death. My job was to make sure all the elements of the three-day Cursillo were carried out in an orderly manner and were true to its purpose and principles. I also gave my testimony on what God had done for my life, making it known that God was the center of my life and that God is good:

Dear Sisters in Christ,

Good afternoon. My name is Tem Villena. I entered my Cursillo in 1982. I came out of the Cursillo with a great mission to evangelize and bring more people to know Christ. My faith in Jesus gave me all the reason to hope for a better spiritual life not only for me but for my whole family. I was able to sustain that feeling of love for a few years until the day of my husband's sudden death on April 30, 1984. We did not even say goodbye. I found myself gradually fading in the darkness, like a plant dying in the hottest desert, thirsty for rain that wasn't there.

The warm feelings of love, the joys of songs and promises, vanished, like the setting of the sun, never, ever to shine again. It was even painful to pray. I was angry with the Almighty for taking my husband away, not only from me but from my small children. I had begun to separate from Him completely. I became a new person, an angry one. My eyes had warped into a miserable black. A look of great bitterness swept across my face every day. Anger was in my gut, like a blazing inferno that wanted to burn me from the inside out, hot and unstoppable. Fear enveloped my being.

Somehow, God did not abandon me but, instead, helped me through the dark, painful nights of grief and showed me the way — the Cursillo way. My Cursillista sisters prayed for me, supported me, and led me back to Jesus. The Cursillo movement helped me, and I started to gain my faith back.

I was once lost, but now I am found. God has given me another chance to be with Him, to know Him, to love Him, and to serve Him. I am blessed.

De colores,
Sis Tem Villena

As the process of healing progressed, I started to break it down like a puzzle. I found the courage to push down deep and entered a personal struggle that had been broken into several million little pieces.

I learned to prioritize the most important steps I needed to heal. I chose them, separated them into compartments, and handled them one at a time. I gradually came up with ideas to solve each one. I added hope, faith, and courage, left out drama and pain, and started to embrace the positive side of life. I finally found the magic of laughter, tranquility, and gratefulness. I found the swords to win — self-love, self-determination, and that magical sensation of well-being. Finally, I was able to face the dragon that had taken residence in my heart and say, "Get out!"

CHAPTER 32

Moving Forward with Flor's Love

The sun shall always rise upon a new day,
and there shall always be a rose garden within me.
Yes, there is always a part of me that is broken,
but my broken soil gives way to my wild roses.

— *C. JoyBell C.*

PEOPLE SAY THAT DEATH plays a natural role in the circle of life, but as anybody who has ever experienced the loss of a loved one will tell you, there is nothing natural about it!

Moving on after the death of my spouse felt like an impossible task — or at least something I would be able to do only in the distant future. I was even finding that a purpose in life seemed impossible. I went through the process of allowing myself to grieve, though grief is not linear. It comes and goes. I did not hurry my grief process.

I started to surround myself with a support system, which helped me a lot. I tried very hard not to make big decisions. I joined a support group to cope with my loss and to find comfort in positive memories. I made sure to take care of myself both physically and mentally. I found myself drinking more water than usual, exercising more, and maintaining my social activities to keep my body strong in order to take care of my children and parents. I started to look forward to the future.

Unfortunately, as we started to heal from Flor's death, life presented other challenges that interrupted the process. My parents were getting old. Tatay Villena passed away after a bout of cancer, which triggered our pain and misery all over again. Our hearts went grieving again because we loved him so much. My sister Bening, the one who stayed to help me, died suddenly, too. Nanay Villena and my mother also passed away. Those deaths left a big scar in our hearts and put our healing on hold. Our hearts were broken into pieces, again and again, pushing our recovery further and further away. To help a little, I wrote farewell notes, which helped ease the pain I had in my heart. This is one of the many letters I wrote, a thank-you letter to Eden, Flor's mother's caregiver:

It has been almost a month since Nanay [Villena] passed, but she continues to come to my dreams.

Nanay has been very good to me. She invited me into her life, and when I came rolling in, she allowed me to unload my heart and bare my true feelings. When my beloved husband passed, Inay carefully poured her blessings over me and showered me with encouragement. When I was scared, she told me how to be strong. She brought blessings into my life and the lives of my children. For that, I am forever grateful. Through the years, I became her daughter, and she became my mother. I love her so much, and I miss her. I miss her terribly. I miss her being a part of my life and her being a part of mine.

Seeing death happen more and more, I began to realize that death is a part of life. Death is not about the body perishing into the Earth; it is about experiencing a journey into the afterlife. If that is the case, then we should not be afraid when it comes. The thought of death comes as a beautiful blessing in the wake of grief.

My children and I have a lot of scars. These scars are reminders that we are the survivors of the deepest wound. Our damaged life left us more robust and more equipped to face the present. These scars are signs of healing and will eventually make us whole again.

The day finally came when V.J. graduated with a degree in sports medicine from the University of San Francisco. I was sure Flor was jumping up and down in heaven. He probably could not believe his boy had finally finished his schooling, although I knew in my heart that he was always keeping an eye on him, and V.J. knew it too. One day, he said, "Mom, I was in the library late at night, and I could not solve a math problem. A guy came to my rescue, and I understood the solution right away. I looked up to say thank you, and he was gone. I just smiled and said to myself, 'Heaven must be in my midst.'"

Remembering his days of not wanting to go to school made me look up to Heaven. I was happy. I was so proud of what he accomplished. After working just a month for John Muir Health, V.J. tried to help his sister Melissa buy a house. I was so glad he was able to do that. I pray every day for my children to get along and always help each other. My gratitude becomes my prayer. I now have two children who finished college.

Rose Jardin, my friend, said, "Tem, one more to go." She was referring to my youngest, Iza.

"I know, one more. I can already see the shore ahead, but I don't know if I can make it there. I am getting so tired, but I will, for sure, give it all of my might," I replied. "Yes, one more kid in college. I am tired but I will swim harder to get her to the shore, never giving up, in spite of everything."

One day, I woke up early. The early-morning daylight, soft and diffuse, gave way to the first intense rays of the day, the ones that bring genuine warmth. In this light, water faded into slow waves, ripples that whirlpool in the gentle breeze, drifting upward to become a flurry of clouds, vessels of white in the blue above. This work of art from the current became stronger, as if the solid and golden rays of the sun were the conductor's baton, and together they called forth the melody of springtide.

I heard the doorbell ring and saw Iza rushing to the foyer with the biggest smile. "Why are you here?" I asked. "Don't you have school?"

"Mom," she excitedly answered, "you can retire now."

"What? Did you win the Lotto?" I asked.

"Mom, come sit down," she said. "I am now a college graduate. I did it in three years."

"Really? I am so proud of you," I answered happily. "How did you do it so fast?"

"I took summer courses, remember?" she answered. "I worked so hard so that you can retire, Mom."

"Wow! Thank you, but I am not at the age to retire yet."

This was a day to remember! God is good. I stopped for a moment and breathed in the fragrance of nature's blossoms because on that day Iza made me so happy. I believed in Iza, knowing that the change would come. She would learn the difference between monsters and angels in her time of transition. Graduating would be a big benefit for her. Working would be so different from college, but she would know I would be there for her no matter what. I could not believe that all of my children were done with college. God was indeed in our midst.

I am mighty proud that all of my children finished college and grew up to be responsible adults. Through all of their growing-up days with me as a single parent, people viewed my children differently. I cried for them because of the hardships they had to go through having just me as a parent. It was nobody's fault that this happened, but other people didn't understand. Being raised well by one parent seems impossible to many, but I discovered that the proper raising of a child does not rely on the structure of the family but rather on the values taught to these children as they learn to mature.

Being a single parent is the most challenging kind of parenting. I tried my best to be both a mother and a father and a good role model. I learned to work hard on my budget because all of the financial responsibilities were on me. Disciplining them also landed on me alone. I did not have Flor to help me out or decide what was wrong or right. I did not know if I could show the gentleness of a mother and the firmness of a father, but I sure tried my best to raise them properly. All parenting responsibilities fell to me — tutor, driver, playmate, housekeeper, problem-solver, caregiver — and my parents. All I know for sure is that I did my best to care for my children. I thank God every day that they all became responsible adults. Looking back, I don't know how we did it, but we did. I am grateful to all of my children for a job well done.

I can gladly say that I did what I had to do with love. I can move forward with the memories I have of Flor. I did what I did because of our love for each other. I can truly say, "Flor, you can be proud of what your children have become."

Epilogue

*We must welcome the future, remembering
that soon it will be the past;
and we must respect the past, remembering
that it was once all that was humanly possible.*

— George Santayana

I FELT COMFORT IN the breeze that wasn't there before. I noticed that the days were becoming lighter and brighter. And then there was the sprout upon the cherry branch, fearless enough to bear such graceful leaves and unfold them into the sunbeams' heaven, which chants of summer song to come. There were the days of cloud rays that made the world so cozy. There were days it began to rain when, instead of sprinting inside, we always stayed in the garden to relish that banquet of water. That was our world. Flor and I were happy with the world, sunlight and rainfall alike. This happiness, I thought, would last forever.

But no. After Flor's death, raising those wide-eyed, perfect, little children became my life's work. The truth was, in many ways, my life had stopped. The one job that was left for me — that little girl flying a paper airplane made of Japanese money, that determined young lady who vowed to be a nurse in spite of everything, that dancer kicking up her heels at the

Fairmont Hotel in San Francisco, that stern head nurse in San Francisco General Hospital — was to hold on for my children, who needed to survive and, if possible, thrive.

Equipped only with great love, faith, and a poem that Flor had left for me, I treaded the uncharted waters of survival along with my children. We each tried very hard to create our own maps, each one unique because we were each special in our experiences and needs. We began to be fine without being all right. We began to unwind instead of shutting down. We were able to let go of the suffering one tiny droplet at a time. Whether it would take days or a lifetime, we saw our emotional wounds begin to fade from red to silver and, though the future was once jet-black, we were beginning to perceive a new day. Our dreams came to keep our flame burning in the freezing wind.

It was not that all things always went right. They didn't, very clearly, and we learned to face that. Yet what we discovered over time was how to make things better, take on board new ways to make changes, and move on. We all promised to work and dream for a better tomorrow before the sun set on us. We learned to ask heaven to guide us on our journey and for the children to dream for a better tomorrow for themselves as well as for their children. We all tried to learn the ways of Heaven and to use our capabilities as best we could.

Terror came to us in rushing waves, so we all learned to swim. This gave us the power to beat fear and welcome our agony as lessons we needed to learn. We chose to march through the flaming inferno to find our promised land. We developed courage, which summoned us to believe and trust.

My children learned to follow their dreams. Melissa and her husband Eddie are following their dreams. Their firstborn son, Nolan, is studying physiological science at the University of California, Los Angeles, with the hope of becoming a doctor someday. Kailyn, their daughter, is taking biological science classes at the University of California, Davis. Their youngest one, Karyssa, is in her second year at Heritage High School in Brentwood, California. V.J., my son, and his wife, Jenny, are also following their dreams. Their daughter, Jordyn, is now in the fifth grade at St. Agnes School in Concord. My youngest daughter, Iza, and her husband, Julien, also have their own dreams to follow with their three children — Jace, Talia, and Selah — all still in elementary school.

My children helped me heal my soul, and my grandchildren have become my crowning glory as I've aged. I am having a grand time watching my children and grandchildren grow to become responsible adults with dreams of their own. We all hold on together with love and respect and trust in our journey of grief. Like a phoenix, we all burned to the ground and then rose from the ashes to fly again.

Acknowledgements

I would like to thank the following people for their help and support:

To **Ashley Mansour**, you always inspire me to continue pursuing my dreams. You have earned my respect and gratitude. Thank you so much for everything.

To **Jacqueline Logue**, my editor, I am forever grateful not only for your brilliant editing but the kindness you have shown me.

To **Kat Pedersen**, my project manager, who is especially kind and patient, thank you for putting up with me.

To **Olivia Robinson**, my book designer, I am forever grateful. You created a beautiful design that captures the eyes of the readers.

To **Arlene Adela Cerda**, my beautiful godchild, thank you for creating a magnificent melody for "The love song from Africa."

For the **Brothers and Sisters in the Cursillo Movement in San Francisco**, I am so thankful for the prayers and your presence in my life. You will always be in my heart.

For **my barkada** (friends), the first and second generations inspire us to get going in *spite* of everything. I am so lucky to have you all in my life. Thank you for your love and concern. You are all in my prayers.

For **Lai, Zeny, Tish, Amy, Fred, and Del**, thank you for being there always in laughter and in pain.

For the **Abcede, Correos, Villena, Conception, Collera, and Garcia families**, thank you for all you do.

To all the **readers**, may you find hope in all of your undertakings and be inspired knowing that life can be beautiful despite all of the obstacles you will face.

About the Author

THELMA GARCIA VILLENA WAS BORN in Manila, Philippines, and graduated from Philippine Women's University in Manila, Philippines. A trained nurse with a bachelor's in the science of nursing, Thelma immigrated to San Francisco from Guam in 1968 and began working at the San Francisco General Hospital as a nurse. She married the love of her life, Florendo Villena, on December 18, 1971, at the St. Gabriel Church in San Francisco. Thelma moved to Concord, California, from San Francisco in 1976. She retired in 2001 at the behest of her youngest daughter, who finished her college degree a year early so Thelma could retire. All of Thelma's children are graduates of the University of San Francisco. Her younger daughter has a degree in psychology, while her son is a graduate of sports medicine, and her eldest daughter graduated with a nursing degree. Thelma enjoys traveling, reading, and writing. Her first book — *Boy, Dream Big* — was an Amazon bestseller and a tribute to her late husband, Florendo Villena.

Rivera Garcia Reunion 2017

My parents, Aguida Rivera Garcia and Timoteo Julian Garcia

Ate Luz, Ate Remy, me, Ate Reming, Sony at the back

The Flor Villena Family

Family photo in front of Waterfront Hotel in Jack London Square, where I got engaged

My Magnificent 7

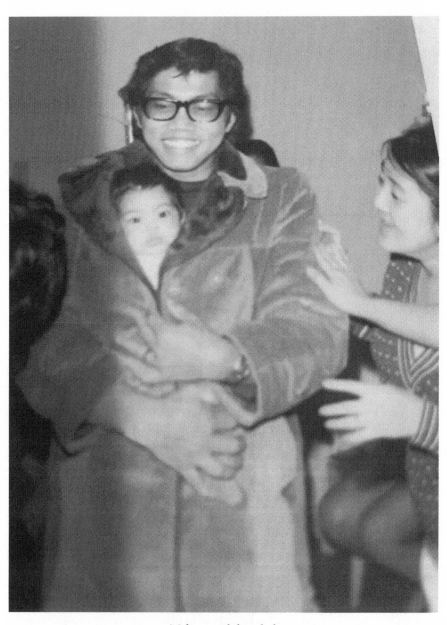

Melissa with her dad

Pappy, Remy, Thelma, and Flor

Friends from SF Cursillo Movement

My Supportive Sisters from SF Cursillo Movement—Sis Bea, Me,
Sis Linda, and Sis Evelyn

Me and my grandkids

Made in the USA
Las Vegas, NV
23 December 2021